Bloom's
GUIDES

F. Scott Fitzgerald's
The Great Gatsby

The Adventures of Huckleberry Finn
All the Pretty Horses
Animal Farm
Beloved
Brave New World
The Chosen
The Crucible
Cry, the Beloved Country
Death of a Salesman
The Grapes of Wrath
Great Expectations
The Great Gatsby
Hamlet
The Handmaid's Tale
The House on Mango Street
I Know Why the Caged Bird Sings
The Iliad
Lord of the Flies
Macbeth
Maggie: A Girl of the Streets
The Member of the Wedding
Of Mice and Men
1984
One Hundred Years of Solitude
Pride and Prejudice
Ragtime
Romeo and Juliet
The Scarlet Letter
Snow Falling on Cedars
A Streetcar Named Desire
The Things They Carried
To Kill a Mockingbird

Bloom's

GUIDES

F. Scott Fitzgerald's
The Great Gatsby

Edited & with an Introduction
by Harold Bloom

BLOOM'S
LITERARY CRITICISM
An imprint of Infobase Publishing

Bloom's Guides: The Great Gatsby

Bloom's Literary Criticism
An imprint of Infobase Publishing
132 West 31st Street
New York NY 10001

ISBN-13: 978-0-7910-8580-6

Library of Congress Cataloging-in-Publication Data

F. Scott Fitzgerald's The Great Gatsby / [introduction by] Harold Bloom.
    p.cm— (Bloom's guides)
    Includes bibliographical references and index.
    ISBN 0-7910-8580-5
    1. Fitzgerald, F. Scott (Francis Scott), 1896–1940. Great Gatsby—Examinations—Study guides. I. Bloom, Harold. II. Series.
    PS3511.I9G8373 2005
    813'.52—dc22   2005031742

Contributing Editor: Gabriel Welsch
Cover design by Takeshi Takahashi

Printed in the United States of America

IBT 10 9 8 7 6 5 4 3

This book is printed on acid-free paper.

Contents

Introduction

HAROLD BLOOM

The Great Gatsby has only a few rivals as the great American novel of the twentieth century; doubtless they would include works by Faulkner, Hemingway, Cather, and Dreiser. Formal shaping is one of the many aesthetic virtues of F. Scott Fitzgerald's masterwork: style, characterization, and plot are all superbly balanced to achieve a highly unified end. Rereading the book, yet once more, my initial and prime reaction is pleasure renewed; it is as though *The Great Gatsby*'s freshness never can wear off. Though it is regarded as the classic of what Fitzgerald himself permanently named the Jazz Age, the novel is anything but a "period piece." Even after many decades, the relevance of *The Great Gatsby* increases, because it is the definitive romance of the American dream, a concept or vision that haunts our society. Critics differ as to whether the theme of the novel is "the withering of the American dream," as Marius Bewley argued, or else a celebration of a Romantic hope in America despite all the ugly realities. Fitzgerald himself, as much a High Romantic as his favorite poet, John Keats, was too great an artist not to entertain both possibilities. In one register, *The Great Gatsby* is a companion work to T.S. Eliot's *The Waste Land*, a desolate vision of a world without faith or order. And yet, in a finer tone, the novel keeps faith with Jay Gatsby's dream of a perfect love, of a fulfillment that transcends the absurdity of Daisy, who in herself is hardly a fit representative of Gatsby's idealized yearnings.

Bewley shrewdly sees Fitzgerald's involvement in Gatsby's aspirations, but again Bewley argues that Gatsby's death is also a spiritual failure. A reader can be legitimately uncertain as to exactly how Gatsby ought to be apprehended. Much depends upon how much the reader places himself under the control of the novel's narrator, Nick Carraway. By mediating Gatsby for us, precisely in the way that Joseph Conrad's Marlow mediates

Jim in *Lord Jim* or Kurtz in *Heart of Darkness*, Carraway's consciousness dominates the novel, and Carraway is no more Fitzgerald than Marlow is Conrad. Marlow's Romanticism is echoed by Carraway's, though Marlow rarely gets in the way of the story's progress, while Carraway frequently does. It is not clear how Fitzgerald wished us to regard Carraway's sometimes less than subtle ironies, but I suspect that they are devices for distancing the novelist from his fictive narrator. Carraway is a very decent fellow, but he does not transcend the fashions of his time and place, as Fitzgerald does. This limitation is one of Carraway's ultimate strengths, because it allows him his own dream of Jay Gatsby as the Romantic hero of the American experience. Fitzgerald, like Conrad before him, regards the deep self as unknowable; Carraway in contrast finds in Gatsby "some heightened sensitivity to the promises of life." The English critic Malcolm Bradbury memorably termed Gatsby "a coarse Platonist" yet any Platonist ultimately is not a materialist. Since Gatsby's dream of love depends upon an alchemy that metamorphoses wealth into eros, we can be reminded of Emerson's wonderful irony: "Money, in some of its effects, is as beautiful as roses."

Gatsby's greatest strength is a "Platonic conception of himself," which gives him the hope that he can roll back time, that he and the unlikely Daisy can somehow be as Adam and Eve early in the morning. Despite the absurd distance of this dream from reality, Gatsby never yields up his hope. That refusal to surrender to reality kills him, yet it also gives him his peculiar greatness, justifying the book's title as being more than an irony. Gatsby's refusal of history is profoundly Emersonian, though doubtless Gatsby had never heard of Emerson. Edith Wharton told Fitzgerald in a letter that "to make Gatsby really great, you ought to have given us his early career." Perhaps, but that is to forget that we know only Carraway's Gatsby, the finished product of an American quest, and a figure curiously beyond Judgment. Actually Fitzgerald had written what we now know as the short story "Absolution" to serve as a picture of Gatsby's early life, but he decided to omit it from the novel so as to preserve some sense of mystery about his hero.

Mystery certainly remains: Gatsby's death, though squalid, transfigures him in the reader's imagination. The dreamer dies so that an image, however grotesque, of the American dream can continue to live. It is not possible that Gatsby dies as a vicarious atonement for the reader, and yet that may be Gatsby's function in regard to Carraway. Nick goes west at the book's conclusion still sustained by the Idealism of Gatsby's effect upon him.

It is one of Fitzgerald's oddest triumphs that we accept his vision of Gatsby's permanent innocence; the gross reality of Daisy's love for her brutal husband, Tom Buchanan, is dismissed by Gatsby as merely "personal" and as something that can be canceled by a simple denial. We come to understand that Gatsby is in love neither with Daisy nor with love itself, but rather with a moment out of time that he persuades himself he shared with Daisy. Gangster and dreamer, Gatsby is more of an inarticulate American poet than he is an episode in the later history of American transcendentalism. Since Fitzgerald is so superbly articulate a writer, Carraway again is necessary as a mediator between the author and his tragic hero. Gatsby's vitalism, his wonderful capacity for hope, is enhanced when Fitzgerald compares him to the endlessly recalcitrant Carraway, whose non-relationship with Jordan Baker heightens our sense of the sexual ambiguity of both characters. What moves Carraway about Gatsby is the image of generosity, of having given oneself away to a dream. Fitzgerald makes us suspect that Gatsby, unlike Carraway, is not deceived altogether by his own dreaming. However inarticulate his own poetic vision is, Gatsby seems to grasp that Daisy indeed is *his* fiction. To believe in your own fiction, while knowing it to be a fiction, is the nicer knowledge of belief, according to Wallace Stevens, who was not being ironic. Gatsby also transcends the ironies of his own story, and so earns his greatness.

Biographical Sketch

Born in St. Paul, Minnesota, on September 24, 1896, to a salesman, Edward, and housewife, Mollie, Francis Scott Fitzgerald developed early on the desire to be a famous writer. During grade school in St. Paul, he wrote plays, songs, poems and the like, gaining him local popularity. In 1911, he was sent east to the Newman School, in Hackensack, New Jersey, and in 1913, he entered Princeton University. Princeton was not the school he had aspired to attend. As a cursory review of his work suggests, he had hoped for Yale. But Princeton, he later said, suited him better. He may have been rationalizing; he was not a good student academically, and never formally graduated. He did excel socially, and saw firsthand at Princeton what Robert Berman notes as the "morally harsh" aspects of American society at the time, and the deep divides along religious, social, economic, and regional lines.

Fitzgerald never graduated, receiving instead a commission in the Army. He never went to war, but he was stationed around the country, most importantly to a base just outside Montgomery, Alabama. The writer and his future wife, Zelda, met at a dance and Fitzgerald was smitten. Some biographers insist that *both* were smitten, but the degree of Zelda's calculation regarding Fitzgerald and whether he had sufficient prospects for long-term earnings is a matter still under debate with Fitzgerald scholars.

Discharged from the Army and dismissed by Zelda as lacking in prospects, Fitzgerald went to New York and worked in advertising so that he could make enough money to justify his pursuit of her. Zelda remained reluctant. Despondent, Fitzgerald returned to St. Paul in 1919 and finished writing *This Side of Paradise*, his first novel. By the end of the year, Scribner and Sons accepted the novel, and Fitzgerald was paired with editor Maxwell Perkins.

Flush with a forthcoming novel and a very good advance, and with his short stories appearing in print and bringing money in, Fitzgerald traveled to New Orleans to write and to pursue Zelda. One week after *This Side of Paradise* was released to acclaim, Zelda and Scott Fitzgerald were wed in the rectory of St. Patrick's Cathedral in New York City.

Later the same year, Fitzgerald's first collection of short stories came out, *Flappers and Philosophers*, also to acclaim. Heralded as a new talent and paid top dollar for his stories, Fitzgerald was on top of the world. He enjoyed the notoriety, the spotlight, and the parties. But he also sought recognition as a major writer, something he thought only his novels would bring. His focus on writing influential novels was so refined that he regarded the majority of the short fiction he wrote—much of it good, some of it mediocre—as hack work completed simply to fund his work on novels. The amounts he received for his short stories were astronomical sums, between $1,000 and $4,000 apiece. The amount is significant even today, but when one considers the real value of the paychecks in 1925 dollars—a $4,000 story would have been equivalent to over $41,000 today—Fitzgerald is among the most lavishly compensated American writers ever to have lived.

He was also one of the most lavish spenders. Fitzgerald was often in debt, asking his agent, Harold Ober, or his editor Max Perkins to advance his next paycheck to cover debts not covered by the last. His early success and his own sense of having to prove his worth, that he had "made it," compelled him to spend, to be conspicuous in his wealth. As a man with the need for both adulation and love, as Mathew Bruccoli has observed, Fitzgerald began to drink heavily in 1920, partly to fuel his own sociability at the parties he attended, partly to steel himself into such sociability, and later to serve his addiction. For a time, he even believed that his writing talent came directly from drink, particularly gin. The partying and heavy borrowing from Perkins and Ober were both trends that would continue for much of Scott Fitzgerald's life.

In 1921, the Fitzgeralds traveled to Europe, visiting France, Italy, and England. They settled in St. Paul, living in an affluent neighborhood. That October, Zelda gave birth to their first and only child, a daughter, Scottie. Fitzgerald wrote a good deal at this time, both stories and a novel. In 1922, both *The Beautiful and the Damned* and *Tales of the Jazz Age* appeared. While 1921 and 1922 were very productive years, they also saw Fitzgerald fighting to find time to write. Though the family lived in St. Paul for most of those years, they held many raucous parties. Fitzgerald also relished his status as local hero, and made much of it. Some have speculated that Zelda, jealous of the attention Fitzgerald gave to his writing, and herself a creature in need of the spotlight, not only supported his drinking to keep him from writing, but engaged in her notorious antics to ensure his attention. Critics and biographers are still divided on just what kind of influence Zelda actually had, and the conversation is particularly heated now that Zelda has her own biographers, scholars, and advocates.

In 1922, the couple moved to Great Neck, the place seen as the inspiration for the fictional West Egg. The Fitzgeralds' party continued, and Scott found himself working harder to find time and solitude such that he needed to write. He wrote a play, *The Vegetable*, published in 1923, and several stories.

In April 1924, the Fitzgeralds departed for France, where Scott began writing *The Great Gatsby*. While there, Zelda started a relationship with a French aviator. While scholars are unsure whether the relationship ever became sexual, they agree it was enough to infuriate Scott and put a rift between himself and Zelda. Some speculate the relationship played a key role in Scott's ideas for *The Great Gatsby*.

Fitzgerald sent the manuscript to Perkins at the end of the summer and revised the novel through the winter of 1924 and 1925. In April 1925, *The Great Gatsby* was released. A month later, Fitzgerald met Ernest Hemingway, and their tumultuous and often contentious friendship began. For Zelda, Hemingway had nothing but antipathy, and the feeling was mutual.

In his biography of Fitzgerald, Bruccoli titles the section containing the years 1925 to 1931, "The Drunkard's Holiday." He had good reason. While Fitzgerald had fits and starts on ideas for novels, wrote portions of *Tender is the Night*, and generally wrote enough stories to get by, the period was marked by the family moving quite a bit, by worrisome declines in Scott's health, and the death of both Scott and Zelda's fathers. As well, in 1930 and 1931, Zelda was institutionalized after a nervous breakdown—resulting from conditions for which she had taken "treatments" several times but which had not, until then, necessitated hospitalization (by standards of the time). While Zelda was in an institution in Nyon, Switzerland, Scott lived and worked nearby, leaving only to attend his father's funeral.

Fitzgerald was not happy with the lukewarm response—critically and financially—to *Gatsby*. He became more and more cynical about writing short stories, despite the success of his collection, *All The Sad Young Men*, released in 1926. The friendship with Hemingway didn't help; Fitzgerald frequently felt inferior to the other man, and let it plague him. Hemingway was not helpful, often castigating Fitzgerald for not focusing on his "true" talent. Hemingway was convinced that much of Fitzgerald's writing was affected.

By 1927, Fitzgerald began work for the movie industry, hoping to be there only briefly and to make enough money to pay off debts and support work on the next project. The family moved to Hollywood, and while he did make some money, when they went to Paris for the summer, Scott mostly drank away the time. Scott returned to movie work at times throughout his life, until he finally died in Hollywood.

In 1932, back in the United States, Zelda had her second breakdown. She was hospitalized at the Phipps Clinic in Baltimore. While in the clinic, Zelda wrote *Save Me The Waltz*, later published by Scribner's the same year. In 1934, writing and edits completed, *Tender is the Night* was serialized in *Scribner's Magazine*, and then published. The next year, Scribner's published *Taps at Reveille*, Fitzgerald's fourth collection of stories.

While other prominent authors wrote to Fitzgerald that they thought *Tender is the Night* was his best yet, the critics and the public did not show similar support. Nor, importantly, did Hemingway. Fitzgerald drank away most of 1934 and 1935.

The only pieces he wrote for the next few years were the essays that comprise *The Crack Up*, and a few abortive attempts at novels.

Through 1937, with Zelda in and out of institutions and Scottie at boarding schools, Fitzgerald went to Hollywood to do more work while trying to write stories to pay his bills. At that time, he met Sheilah Graham, the woman with whom he would have a devoted affair until he died. Scott and Zelda's marriage effectively dissolved through atrophy, recrimination over her sickness, the handling of Scottie, and Scott's prolonged absences. By late 1937, Scott became a resident, however peripatetic, of California. Through the winter of 1937 and 1938, he worked on a movie script and earned his single film credit. He worked for MGM until, at the end of 1938, his contract was not renewed. He freelanced for several studios, even working briefly on *Gone with the Wind*, but was never regularly employed by a studio again.

Bruccoli points out that Fitzgerald was "happy" with Graham—to the point that he stopped drinking for a while. Bruccoli cites Graham's own assessment that of the forty-two months they were together, he only drank during nine of them. However, when he did drink, he would often become belligerent or even violent. By summer 1939, Harold Ober dropped Fitzgerald as a client, having lost faith in the writer's ability to write reliably. Scott sold a few things on his own, including a series of stories to *Esquire*. He also wrote most of *The Last Tycoon*, his so-called "Hollywood novel," and in December 1940, died of a heart attack in Sheilah Graham's apartment. *The Last Tycoon* and *The Crack Up* each were published posthumously.

The Story Behind the Story

T.S. Eliot labeled *The Great Gatsby* "the first step that American fiction has taken since Henry James." Such praise was exactly what Fitzgerald hoped for, as his letters to Maxwell Perkins make clear. It would not be the case. Many critics failed to understand what Fitzgerald had attempted with *The Great Gatsby*, focusing more on what they felt was lurid content rather than engaging the themes of the book. The book sold respectably, but not well. At the time of Fitzgerald's death, most of the second printing remained in the Scribner's warehouse.

The roots of the story go back deep in Fitzgerald's early life. In 1914, home in St. Paul from Princeton for the Christmas holiday, Fitzgerald met Ginevra King, a daughter of a socially prominent St. Paul family and the object of many suitors. The early encounter of Gatsby and Daisy is a stylized and romanticized version of Fitzgerald and King's early encounters. Like Gatsby, Fitzgerald meets King at a time when his prospects are far better than his actual standing. Ginevra also has many suitors. Just as Gatsby had to leave and soon went to war, so, too, did Fitzgerald return to Princeton and, in 1917, take his commission as a 2nd lieutenant in the U.S. Army.

The moment stayed with him. Fitzgerald had always been susceptible to romantic notions. Like Gatsby, Scott Fitzgerald kept lists in his own journals, lists of steps to take for self-improvement. He put daydreams on paper about being a famous novelist and influential man. And, like Gatsby, he went far from home and, to some degree, borrowed a personality in order to realize his dreams.

Daisy Buchanan is seen by many as a conflation of Ginevra King and Zelda Sayre. Daisy's zeal for the gesture and antics of being drunk owes much to Zelda's behavior, as well as the behavior of many around the Fitzgeralds. As well, Gatsby's parties were only slightly hyperbolic representations of the chaos that abounded in Great Neck, the inspiration for West Egg.

But while he had the material all around him, Fitzgerald was not driven as much by his experiences as by his ideas for the novel. With two novels and two short story collections under his belt, he wanted to try something new—an intricate and layered novel whose prose technique would separate it from other writing popular at the time.

In June 1922, he already knew his next novel would be different. He wrote to Perkins that "It will concern less superlative beauties than I run to usually." By April of 1924, he had a very good idea of what he would do, writing to Perkins, "in approaching it from a new angle I've had to discard a lot of it—in one case 18,000 words." The discarded piece formed the short story, "Absolution," a story critics agree is an early study of the character of Jay Gatsby. Fitzgerald himself indicated it was to have been the "prologue." Perkins' response mentions the title, "The Great Gatsby," which he says is "a suggestive and effective title,—with only the vaguest knowledge of the book, of course." In other words, Fitzgerald exhibited the classic signs of a writer who knew he was on to something: he said little.

When Perkins received the first draft, titled on the manuscript "Trimalchio at West Egg," he wrote to Fitzgerald, "you have every kind of right to be proud of this book." He pointed out some strengths—particularly the narrative mode and the use of symbol in the book. At the same time, he felt Gatsby was too vague. Fitzgerald appreciated the insight as well as the support. He noted that Perkins "picked out all [his] favorite spots in the book to praise as high spots. Except you didn't mention my favorite of all—the chapter where Daisy and Gatsby meet."

In the letters the two exchanged in the last months of 1924 and into 1925, too lengthy to quote from here, Fitzgerald's purpose and acumen are clear. They show how much thought he had given to every move in the novel, to every bit of language, to the layers and complications he had stated, early on, that he wanted.

Many scholars—but chiefly Matthew Bruccoli and Scott Donaldson—have outlined the numerous parallels between

Fitzgerald's life and many elements of the novel. The most obvious parallels come in the character of Daisy Buchanan and her interactions with Jay Gatsby. But the letters between Perkins and Fitzgerald make clear many more—from the real-life source for Jordan Baker to the likely source for Tom Buchanan, from the inclusion of Robert Keable's *Simon Called Peter* to the source for Gatsby's obscure medal.

Though the novel produced mediocre reviews and sales in its time, there were a few who knew its importance. As Perkins wrote to Fitzgerald after reading and thinking about that first draft: "You once told me you were a natural writer—my God! You have plainly mastered the craft, of course; but you needed far more than craftsmanship for this."

List of Characters

Nick Carraway narrates the story of *The Great Gatsby* as he recalls the events of the novel from two years afterward. After moving to West Egg to be out of New York but still close enough to work there as a money manager, he rents a house directly next door to Jay Gatsby. His perspective of the novel's events is colored by his feelings of difference and absence in comparison to that of the rich characters as well as by the spectacle of Gatsby's tragic quest for Daisy.

Daisy Buchanan, Nick's distant cousin, is married to Tom Buchanan. She is described variously as a socially adept but cynical woman, a smart but typical flapper, a girl with "a voice full of money." Jay Gatsby met her once and began a romance, but the romance ebbed and Daisy married Tom Buchanan.

Tom Buchanan, Daisy's husband, is having an affair with Myrtle Wilson, the wife of a garage owner whose dingy shop is located in the "valley of ashes" between Manhattan and the fashionable communities of East and West Egg. Tom is described as cold, forceful, arrogant, and affluent.

Myrtle Wilson loathes her mechanic husband, **George**. She has an affair with Tom Buchanan and is portrayed as thick and pompous. Ultimately, she is killed when Daisy, while driving Jay Gatsby's car, accidentally hits her in the valley of ashes. George seeks out and kills Gatsby, thinking Gatsby Myrtle's lover and murderer.

Jordan Baker is a golf-pro who attends Gatsby's parties and meets Nick at the Buchanans' early in the novel. While living largely at the expense of the Buchanans, Jordan is frequently Nick's guide through the labyrinths of excess that characterize Gatsby's parties, and asks Nick to arrange for Gatsby to surprise Daisy. Jordan and Nick pursue a brief love affair.

Jay Gatsby is the assumed name of the young affluent who owns the sprawling house on West Egg next to which Nick Carraway lives and to which hordes of Manhattan socialites flock each Friday night for over-the-top parties. Gatsby throws elaborate parties held solely to attract Daisy Buchanan to attend them. Gatsby's hope is to rekindle a long lost romance with Daisy.

Summary and Analysis

Over nine chapters, F. Scott Fitzgerald constructed a novel that he once confessed in a letter sounded almost like pulp when one simply wrote down the bones of the story. Jimmy Gatz falls in love with Daisy, a young woman from a wealthy family, but at the time lacks the financial resources and confidence in his past necessary to propose marriage. He leaves then, determined to make his fortune that he may return to marry her and support her in a manner reasonable for her expectations and her class. He changes his name to Jay Gatsby, earns his fortune through illicit means, bootlegging and organized gambling, and as he earns it so quickly, he is not in possession of the bearing and mores to handle wealth to which so many of Daisy's suitors were born. His house, his clothing, his car—all scream of his "new" wealth, making his wealth less alluring than that of "old money."

In the quest to lure Daisy to him, he purchases a home near hers and begins to throw enormous parties, solely meant to attract her interest, such that she would eventually stroll into his home during one of his parties, discover him, and fall in love all over again. Instead, Nick Carraway, Daisy's second cousin, moves in next door. When Gatsby realizes the family relationship, he asks Nick to help him "accidentally" encounter Daisy again. When Nick does, Gatsby learns Daisy is unhappily married to Tom Buchanan, a rich boor. Daisy is impressed with the things Gatsby has amassed. However, Daisy is also fickle, unpredictable, and more complicated than Jay Gatsby assumes. As well, her marriage to Tom provides her benefits and comforts Gatsby does not and, due to the limits of his experience, cannot understand.

After Tom confronts Gatsby during a drunken lark in the Plaza Hotel in Manhattan, everyone leaves in separate cars. Daisy and Gatsby race back in his car and, with Daisy driving, they strike down and kill a woman coming out to meet them, Myrtle Wilson, Tom's vapid and déclassé mistress. Daisy and

Gatsby drive away, not even stopping. Myrtle's husband, George, is immediately distraught, so much so that he becomes murderous. Having seen the car earlier, and knowing Tom through his garage business, George finds out who owned the atypical car. George then hunts down and kills Gatsby. In the denouement, no one attends Gatsby's funeral except his decrepit father, Nick, and a senile partygoer. Daisy and Tom travel abroad. George Wilson goes to jail. Nick moves on, with the realization that dreams, even malformed dreams such as Jay Gatsby's, drive us against the unknown world.

Of course, the novel contains far, *far* more than the just-mentioned elaborate series of events. Fitzgerald himself wrote to Maxwell Perkins, his famous editor at Scribner's, that it was his intent to write an intricately crafted novel along the lines of his heroes, Conrad and Thackeray, and one that would be wholly different than anything that had come before. Other critics say that Conrad is not exactly the right stylistic antecedent. To them, Henry James would be more appropriate, given James' weaving of essential—and only essential—details. But the critics have long argued about Gatsby's stylistic antecedents, due to its complex layers and its universality. But the text of *The Great Gatsby* gives even the casual reader much to think about, so dense is its structure, so distinctive is its language, so full is its plot, and so effortless it all appears.

Epigraph and Chapter One

Though attributed to Thomas Parke D'Invilliers, Fitzgerald himself actually wrote the novel's epigraph. As a statement fronting the book, it could have been instructions given to Jimmy Gatz on how to approach the one for which he pined:

> *Then wear the gold hat, if that will move her;*
> *If you can bounce high, bounce for her too,*
> *Till she cry "Lover, gold-hatted, high-bouncing lover*
> *I must have you!"*

In other words, do what you must, young Gatz. Earn gold, dance, what have you. If you do the things she likes, she will be yours. The advice presupposes a degree of formulaic demeanor on the part of the one pursued, and so is a kind of antiquated bit of advice when compared with what Gatz and Buchanan and Carraway would have understood about affluent young women of the 1920s.

By 1925, Fitzgerald had earned a reputation as a trustworthy first chronicler of the "flapper," a young woman who chafed against the prohibitions of the period, who danced and wore revealing clothes and frequented speakeasies, and who, while certainly swayed by a number of influences, was often also purposefully contrary, argumentative, and willful. The popular literature of the period either dealt with flappers salaciously, as temptresses whose loose morality would be the undoing of society, or—as did Fitzgerald and a few others—as women whose exposure to modern wealth, disillusionment, achievement, art, and other aspects of worldly culture inspired them to break with convention, to varying results. In some cases, it led to women whose very complication of character would seem scandalous to people still accustomed to typical Victorian and Romantic portrayals of women. To others, the complexity of a so-called flapper was the embodiment of the times having changed, the advent of modernity. Thus, Fitzgerald knew, while such feats as high-bouncing and wearing a gold hat might impress a young woman of the time, she was just as likely to leave a young man on his own at the end of the evening, or to kiss another man in the very next dance.

So the advice comes from someone antiquated by comparison, some name that sounds neither "American" (in the narrow way Tom Buchanan might interpret the word) nor modern: Thomas Parke D'Invilliers, a name that sounds as though it belonged to a stuffed-shirt poet of the Victorian era—and certainly not a modern man, one who understands the industrial age and the changing face of everything when cast against the great doubt and wasteland created in the aftermath of the Great War.

The certainty of the epigraph almost immediately rubs up against the moral and spiritual uncertainty pervading the novel itself. Chapter One opens with Nick Carraway introducing the story to readers, while first introducing himself, and telling how he, a person of solid Midwestern upbringing, happened to fall in with a crowd of eastern decadents. He begins asserting that he is careful to criticize, and while he explains why, the explanation also provides a clue into why he is the perfect narrator for the story. He says, "I'm inclined to reserve all judgments, a habit that has opened up many curious natures to me." As we see throughout the novel, Nick does inspire people to moments of candor, of confession, such that he is not only a witness, he is the only person privy to the real characters of the individuals he encounters.

Nick's explanation and constant qualification of how he came to be in the East ("my aunts and uncles talking it over as if they were choosing a prep school for me, and finally said, 'Why ye-es,' with very grave, hesitant faces ... the Middle West now seemed like the ragged edge of the universe—") also serves to give readers a sense of the trauma to come. Nick's foreboding narration gives immediate tension to the tale, particularly as much of the foreboding is centered on the first mention of Gatsby.

Gatsby, even two years after the fact, had "something gorgeous about him." And if Nick is now sour on the East and its "riotous excursions," it is for no fault of Gatsby's. Rather, Nick has seen a heart of darkness, of sorts. For Fitzgerald's hero, Conrad, the heart of darkness was a similar thing: a perverse extreme of human nature. For Fitzgerald, through the cipher of Nick Carraway, the perversion in this case was "what preyed on Gatsby, what foul dust floated in the wake of his dreams that temporarily closed out [Nick's] interest in the abortive sorrows and short-winded elations of men." Fitzgerald does not have Nick tell the reader yet what it is; the answer is complicated, and requires the story. It is not simply affluence, nor is it moral decay in the face of fatalism. Neither is it aspiration; although, for Nick, Gatsby's acquisitive zeal and corruptibility by wealth and status turned him into a man "who represented everything for which I have an unaffected scorn," the man himself still possessed "an extraordinary gift for hope, a romantic readiness such as I have never found in any other person and which it is not likely I will ever find again." Unlike all the other characters Nick met, Gatsby had hope.

Nick details the business circumstances that resulted in his being in West Egg, as opposed to the more fashionable East Egg. West Egg was the nouveau riche locale, and East Egg had old mansions of older money. Gatsby, of course, lived at West Egg. The Buchanans lived at East Egg. Nick rented one of the few remaining small houses left on West Egg. Outside the city, in the Long Island communities housing the social elite, Nick finds promise: "I had the familiar conviction that life was beginning over again with summer." Fitzgerald's style mirrors Nick's feeling through metaphor: "so much fine health to be pulled down out of the young breath-giving air."

Soon, Nick describes Gatsby's mansion, an enormous anachronistic palace, gaudy even for the time, a decade or two previous, when it would have been the style, part of a late nineteenth-century revival of Gothic and Roman architecture. The description reveals its vulgarity: "factual imitation," "a tower on one side, spanking new under a thin beard of raw ivy." As well, Nick tells about East Egg, and the "white palaces"— marking the beginning of Fitzgerald's constant use of color, particularly white, to indicate status. White—as well as gold and silver—are almost exclusively used throughout *The Great Gatsby* to signal an ethereal affluence.

Nick introduces Tom before he does Daisy, perhaps because Tom is an easier person for Nick to nail down in a few words. Tom is an athletic sort, at one time a famous football player at Yale. But his glory days have passed; Nick says he was "one of those men who reach such an acute limited excellence at twenty-one that everything afterward savors of anticlimax." In other words, Tom peaked early in life. But he is wealthy, enough to buy polo ponies, spend a year idling in France, do things which make Nick find it "hard to realize that a man in my own generation was wealthy enough to do."

As Nick approaches the Buchanans' house for the first major scene of the novel, and the scene that dominates Chapter One, the prose grows more unusual in spots, marking moments in which Fitzgerald sought the reader's high engagement, a stylistic choice examined in more detail by Jackson R. Bryer. Bryer points out how Fitzgerald paired adjectives and adverbs with nouns and verbs in very unexpected combinations, thereby surprising readers and demanding their heightened attention to the prose and its suggestive qualities. The effect, according to Bryer, is to not only make the prose very active and distinctive, but to suggest the amplified and distinct quality of the novel's settings.

Stylistic innovation and color both are very much at work in the first section: the house is red and white, the front yard features "burning gardens," and Tom Buchanan stands, legs apart like a colossus, on the porch, surveying his domain as he awaits Nick. Tom is then described in a paragraph featuring such modifiers as "hard," "supercilious," "arrogant," "dominance," "aggressively," "power," and "cruel." The surprising pairing of "pack" and "muscle" gives Tom Buchanan bulk and presence as a character, particularly one standing at the edge of a lawn that metaphorically burns, in a house where the lawn "jumps" up the sides in "bright vines."

Tom's strength is something of an act. Nick notes Tom's need for approval, that Tom wanted Nick to like him "with some harsh, defiant wistfulness" (another unusual grouping of words). Tom declares to Nick that he has a "nice place here," rather than asking Nick's opinion. Tom's strength, his home, his rude superiority and his almost brittle need for approval combine to suggest the conflicts at work within him, conflicts with consequences for the plot of *The Great Gatsby*.

Once the two men enter the house, into "rosy-colored space," everything is in motion, a device used by Fitzgerald in many scenes involving the Buchanans and their friends. In the home, a breeze works through the room, curtains rise. Grass seems to grow into the house, and the reiteration of white colors dresses, the "wedding-cake" ceiling, the windows, and more. Tom puts a stop to the motion by shutting the windows with a "boom"; the action is the first of many wherein Tom will change the quality of a room or a moment. In the absence of all the motion, Nick's attention is drawn to Daisy and Jordan, both in white.

Jordan is described as someone attempting to balance an object on her chin, almost as though she were a statue. Jordan's posture and aspect suggest an almost Petrarchan treatment. Daisy, on the other hand, is motion and self-awareness, a spirit of contradiction from the first moment. Her expression is "conscientious," and she makes an "absurd, charming little laugh," and declares, with the intent to ingratiate herself to whomever she meets, "I'm p-paralyzed with happiness." Daisy herself is the only one who laughs at her comment, "as if she said something very witty."

Through Nick's introduction of Daisy, Fitzgerald is able to use his narrator to distinct advantage. Rather than simply let the scene occur in the present tense, dramatized so that the reader interprets the actions, Fitzgerald has Nick report about it from the standpoint of looking back, knowing how to guide us. With a character like Daisy, someone so adept at charming people, it is helpful and important (in this case) to have a narrator who can help the reader deduce Daisy's character. Thus, when Daisy greets Nick, holding his hand and "looking up into [his] face, promising there was no one in the world she so much wanted to see," he can tell the reader, frankly, "That was a way she had." When she murmurs Jordan's last name, he notes, "I've heard it said that Daisy's murmur was only to make people lean toward her; an irrelevant criticism that made it no less charming."

Fitzgerald makes much of Daisy's voice throughout the novel. Nick finds it charming, engaging, and it is her most compelling characteristic—despite what Nick tells us is her great beauty:

I looked back at my cousin, who began to ask me questions in her low, thrilling voice. It was the kind of voice that the ear follows up and down, as if each speech is an arrangement of notes that will never be played again. Her face was sad and lovely with bright things in it, bright eyes and a bright passionate mouth, but there was an excitement in her voice that men who had cared for her found difficult to forget: a singing compulsion, a whispered 'Listen,' a promise that she had done gay, exciting things just a while since and that there were gay, exciting things hovering in the next hour.

Daisy is, for Nick, for Tom, for Gatsby, promise, an entirety of light and delight not fully attainable. She is also self-indulgent, flirtatious, and fragile. As she jokes with Nick about Chicago and how everyone misses her, she refers once to her child, a three-year-old daughter, and Tom breaks into the discussion only to compare vocations with Nick. When Tom hears that Nick works in bonds, he dismisses the narrator's firm "decisively." When Nick says that Tom will soon know the firm if he stays in the East, Tom declares he'd be "a God damned fool to live anywhere else."

The scene moves on through a number of details that, to individuals not living in locales like East Egg and working in Manhattan in the 1920s, would seem frivolous, decadent, immoral, or worse. Tom curses. He takes a drink as if "it were a drop in the bottom of a glass," an important detail during Prohibition and amidst widespread temperance movements left over from the period after the Civil War. In Chapter Two, the violence is fueled by two bottles of whiskey, and the series of missteps in Chapter Seven are similarly instigated. The presence of booze throughout the book would have provoked responses ranging from recognition to shock. The amounts of money referred to would also have been exorbitant; in Chapter Two, Myrtle Wilson's sister, Catherine, mentions losing $1,200 in two days while traveling in Europe. Given that most Americans of typical means in 1925 had never left the state in which they lived, and they made scarcely more than $1,200 per year, both details would have revealed a world of privilege as alien as the surface of the moon. Jordan Baker complains of lounging the afternoon away on the couch, whereas most Americans at the time would have been working six or seven days a week, and leisure time would have been largely unheard of.

While much about Daisy and Tom is colored in white or shades of red, Jordan Baker is drawn as "gray," "sun-strained," with a "wan, charming, discontented face." Jordan is different from the Buchanans in that she is not a celebrity due to society or generations of wealth, and her demeanor and description supports it. She is, Nick learns, a professional athlete, and so is still part of the society of affluence and leisure, but of a lesser level than the wealthy Buchanans.

The conversation turns to Gatsby, but is cut short by dinner, through which Tom sulks and launches into a boorish conversation on race and supremacy which he instigates after taking umbrage at Daisy's referring to him as a "brute of a man, a great, big, hulking physical specimen." When Tom is called from the table to answer the phone, Daisy works to charm Nick some more, until she, too, leaves to follow Tom. At that point, Jordan tells Nick, "Tom's got some woman in New York."

When Daisy and Tom return, Daisy announces her departure "couldn't be helped." She does so with "tense gayety"—another startling pairing of words—after which she forces the conversation toward what she might show Nick, if there is enough light after dinner. But as the conversation has proceeded, the light has steadily left the room. As Nick puts it, it is as though the light is leaving Daisy herself: "each light deserting her with lingering regret, like children leaving a pleasant street at dusk." As the light leaves, so, too, does her attitude change. As the twilight moves in, and candles wink out, Daisy tells Nick, finally, "I've had a very bad time, Nick, and I'm pretty cynical about everything."

Her admission colors the reader's understanding of the ferocity of her charm. To use the modern language of pop psychology, one might accuse Daisy of living in willful denial of her situation in front of others, and of only facing the reality of her situation when her defenses are down. With Daisy, however, such analysis is not that simple. As Nick suggests, even when she is being forthright about her life, it could also be another part of her arsenal of tools with which to charm. When she confesses how alone she felt at the birth of her daughter, when Tom was nowhere to be found, she tells Nick that she hoped her daughter would grow into a "fool—that's the best thing a girl can be in this world, a beautiful little fool."

Daisy's cynicism is also a bit fashionable, as she herself points out. However real the sense of disillusionment was amongst the generation that fought in and returned from World War I (and about which Malcolm Cowley and Ernest Hemingway wrote most memorably in *Exile's Return* and *A Moveable Feast*, respectively), many also flocked to the fashionable and iconoclastic position of cynicism in the face of a burgeoning American economy based on the strong pseudo-secular zeal of the Protestant work ethic. Sinclair Lewis's *Main Street* and *Babbitt* were published while Fitzgerald was writing, and as his characters were not quite as far in the fringe as were Fitzgerald's disaffected affluents, Lewis won more acclaim, more attention, and more readers than Fitzgerald. But they underscore a point to which Fitzgerald also wrote: disaffection and cynicism were rampant among the culturally elite. What separates Fitzgerald from Lewis is that the former's work looks at the disillusionment itself and its effect, whereas the latter's produces art from the standpoint of cynicism. Some critics argue the difference is precisely why Lewis is no longer much read today, whereas the popularity of Fitzgerald's work endures.

Daisy's possible faddishness is revealed in her overwrought exclamation to Nick:

"You see I think everything's terrible anyhow," she went on in a convinced way. "Everybody thinks so—the most advanced people. And I *know*. I've been everywhere and seen everything and done everything." Her eyes flashed around her in a defiant way, rather like Tom's, and she laughed with thrilling scorn. "Sophisticated—God, I'm sophisticated!"

Daisy compares herself to Tom: she wants everyone to think her sophisticated in the same way Tom wants everyone to think him rich and powerful. Daisy is, as Nick says, convinced in the way that the desperate are convinced: she has averred her own sophistication for so long that she has come to believe her own hype.

And it is hype. As Nick points out, once Daisy stops speaking, he is no longer compelled. He feels the "basic insincerity of what she had said." At that moment, Nick feels quite forcefully the gap between himself and the Buchanans, and it is a foreshadowing of the increasing isolation he will feel from everyone else in the novel. Daisy looks at Nick and he sees her assert "her membership in a rather distinguished secret society to which she and Tom belonged." And one to which Nick most assuredly does not belong.

When Nick returns home, he sees Gatsby for the first time. He mistakenly thinks his neighbor is looking at the stars. Gatsby's posture impresses Nick, as he seems comfortable, sure, even graceful. Then, Gatsby does something surprising that arrests Nick's attention: "he stretched his eyes toward the dark water in a curious way, and, far as I was from him, I could have sworn he was trembling." Nick only sees a green light, the light readers later learn shines from the end of the Buchanans' dock.

Chapter Two

Chapter Two details Nick's foray into the city with Tom and his mistress and the drunken shenanigans that ensue. It features several layers Fitzgerald constructs to develop important symbols and plot details.

The first few paragraphs introduce readers to two of the most enduring symbols in *The Great Gatsby*: the valley of the ashes and the eyes of Dr. T.J. Eckleburg. The valley of ashes is "that solemn dumping ground," the industrial stretch between East and West Egg and Manhattan, where everything is gray. Nick says the ash forms "grotesque gardens," taking shape as "houses and chimneys and rising smoke and, finally, with a transcendent effort, of ash-gray men who move dimly and already crumbling through the powdery air." It is a stylized depiction of the neighborhoods and blocks where working people—those who are not of Daisy and Tom's "distinguished secret society," or even of Nick's own class—live. The bleakness and despondency of their lives and fates, as perceived by Nick and others, are the realities from which Gatsby himself had fled. The ordinary is thus conceived of as horrific, crumbling, hopeless—quotidian with fatal verve. Queens is, then, neither the ribald bustle of Manhattan nor the moneyed enclave of the Eggs. It is drudgery, where fire's only evidence is the ash left after consumption. If there is any question as to the importance of the symbol to the novel, consider that one of Fitzgerald's several working titles for the novel was "Among Ash Heaps and Millionaires."

The valley of ashes powders under the watchful eyes of Dr. T.J. Eckleburg. Long ago erected by "some wild wag of an oculist" to "fatten his practice in the boroughs of Queens," the eyes of the doctor "brood" like those of a despondent god. George Wilson later sees them almost literally as the eyes of God. They are also ever seeing, overseeing, never blinking, and take the role of conscience, witness, and judge.

Because a "small foul river" (or, the East River) borders the valley, the train into the city is often delayed at the drawbridge, making passengers "stare at the dismal scene for as long as half an hour." That delay, Nick tells the reader, resulted in his meeting Tom Buchanan's mistress. The two had been heading into New York when they hit the delay and, rather than waiting, Tom suddenly says, "I want you to meet my girl." He "literally forced" Nick off the train and the two walk along "under Doctor Eckleburg's persistent stare." The stare comes after Tom's brazen admission to a mistress, and watches Nick's (however reluctant) complicity in going to meet the woman.

They end up at George Wilson's garage, described as "unprosperous and bare," in stark contrast to the sumptuous animation of the Buchanan home. It is a "shadow of a garage," another contrast to the light constantly surrounding Daisy and Tom. George Wilson himself wipes his hand on "a piece of waste," is a "spiritless man, anæmic [sic]," and when he sees the two, "a damp gleam of hope sprang" into his eyes.

The short conversation that follows reveals that Tom is trying to sell a car to Wilson, entering them into a business arrangement crucial to the later plot. The remarks are almost lost as an aside, and are a very good example of how densely Fitzgerald had packed the short novel. Every piece of each

31

chapter is critical to the plot or the full understanding of the characters, even though the importance is seldom apparent at the time of its mention. To someone reading the book for the first time, the conversation between Tom and George may seem incidental, little more than small talk about an unrelated fact of their acquaintance, but it is their potential business interaction that leads George, through other connections and actions, finally to kill Gatsby.

Myrtle Wilson's presence contrasts forcefully with Daisy Buchanan's. She literally "blocks out the light," carries "surplus flesh sensuously," and her face "contained no facet or gleam of beauty." But where Daisy is charm and illusion, lightness and façade, Myrtle Wilson has "an immediately perceptible vitality about her as if the nerves of her body were continually smouldering." The reasons for Tom's attraction are underscored by Fitzgerald's use of fire imagery in the initial description of both characters. For Tom, it was the burning gardens. With Myrtle, it is her smoldering of vitality. Although she and her husband are rendered separately from the Buchanans by color (for each, the only color mentioned is blue), Myrtle is differentiated from George by her stunning substance. She walks through "her husband as if he were a ghost" and orders him around, clearly dominating him.

As George moves to get chairs, Nick notes the "white ashen dust" covering his shoulders, linking the dust, perhaps, to the Buchanans and their ilk. The valley of ashes is covered in the ash drifting down from on high, from the fiery consumption of the elite. It veils everything, Nick notes. The effect of the wealthy covers everyone else in a fine scrim.

Nick and Tom leave after Tom tells Myrtle to get on a train, to meet him in the city. Tom denounces the entire place outside, and as he does so, meets the eye of Eckleburg again, "exchanging a frown." Since the eyes have no corresponding face, or even any other features, the characters are free to imagine the expression such a face might have, projecting their own assumptions on God, after a fashion. The only characters in the novel that make that assumption, however, are also the most desperate ones: Wilson, Tom, and Gatsby.

The use of color and characterization continues in the scene which follows, wherein Tom and Myrtle meet in New York. Myrtle wears a brown dress, picks up a copy of *Town Tattler*, a rough equivalent to today's *Star* magazine, or *Us Weekly*, a tabloid that, in its day, followed the exploits of Broadway and the fledgling movie industry, then still centered in New York. The cab she selects is lavender (a variation on blue) with gray upholstery. She chatters about getting a dog for the apartment. In all aspects, she reveals her station as below that of the Buchanans (who, rather than *Town Tattler*, read George Horace Lorimer's vastly superior *Saturday Evening Post*, the magazine of national conversation, and one in which Fitzgerald himself had published many of his stories and in which he later serialized *Tender is the Night*).

Once the trio makes it to Fifth Avenue, the city is "warm and soft, almost pastoral" and Nick says, "I wouldn't have been surprised to see a great flock of white sheep," underscoring again the contrast between the realm of wealth (the Eggs and Manhattan) and the valley of ashes. Several of Nick's later depictions of the city have similar qualities. At the same time, Myrtle's displacement regarding her station continues to be clear; she mentions her sister Catherine and announces, "she's said to be very beautiful by people who ought to know." In her zeal for such approval, she appears for a moment to be similar to Daisy. But unlike Daisy, cynicism does not undercut Myrtle's zeal.

The apartment's details include more copies of *Town Tattler*, as well as a copy of *Simon Called Peter*, a 1921 novel by Robert Keable. Fitzgerald had called the novel "immoral" and a "piece of trash" in *The New York Herald* in March 1923, and its inclusion is meant to imply the same about Myrtle Wilson. In addition to the reading material, Nick notices a single picture, "an over-enlarged photograph, apparently a hen sitting on a blurred rock." As he looks at it, though, it dissolves, and readers learn it resembles a famous optical illusion—resonating with the illusory quality of Myrtle's aspirations to culture. That the illusion is really Myrtle's mother is yet another layer of revelation.

Nick is soon drunk on Tom's whiskey, but notes that it was

only the second time he had ever been drunk. And that he has not been drunk since. The admission is another instance wherein Fitzgerald's construction of a narrator is apparent and important. The admission, in the present tense, indicates that throughout the remainder of the events of the novel, many of which transpire in liquor-soaked afternoons and parties, Nick is sober, and thus reliable, insofar as his biases allow. As well, it reinforces how he is separate from the other individuals in the novel. His honesty and isolation are so important to his credibility that Fitzgerald asserts them on occasion throughout the book, but perhaps most memorably at the end of Chapter Three, when Nick notes—believably—"I am one of the few honest people that I have ever known." (It is also notable that Nick rarely places himself in situations wherein he might be compelled to dishonesty.)

Company starts to arrive, and Myrtle's sister Catherine is "a sticky bob of red hair, and a complexion powdered milky white." A pure flapper, her arms bangle with bracelets, and her coloring matches that of Tom and Daisy. The only difference is that it is clearly cultivated: the bob is sticky, as if colored, and the complexion is created with powder. She is proprietary, possessive, acquisitive—in all, a more refined version of her sister. Myrtle, by the time company arrives, is wearing cream. It's not white, but she is approaching the palette of the elite, and it rustles, appropriating the movement more typical to both Jordan and Daisy.

The McKees arrive as well. He is a photographer, the one who took the photo of Myrtle's mother, and is, like George, dominated by his carping wife. As the conversation progresses, Catherine asks Nick if he knows Gatsby. She tells him that people think Gatsby is a descendant of Kaiser Wilhelm, the ruler of Germany before and during World War I. It is the first of many rumors Nick will hear about his neighbor. Many critics have written about how Fitzgerald's decision to delay the truth about Gatsby's past contributes to the novel's tension and makes Gatsby the memorable character he becomes.

As Catherine tells Nick about how neither Myrtle nor Tom

could stand their spouses, Myrtle overhears and soon launches into a classist tirade about how George fooled her into marrying her: "I thought he knew something about breeding, but he wasn't fit to lick my shoe." As the whiskey continues to flow, Nick tries to leave, but continues to become "entangled in some wild, strident argument." He is aware of his observation as well as his complicity in the excess. Nick's conflict over his own difference stirs in him:

> Yet high over the city our line of yellow windows must have contributed their share of human secrecy to the casual watcher in the darkening streets, and I was him too, looking up and wondering. I was within and without, simultaneously enchanted and repelled by the inexhaustible variety of life.

The night winds down—McKee is asleep, the dog stares off, people move in and out—and yet the tension rises between Myrtle and Tom, as both are aware of transgression and frustration, when near midnight they begin to argue over whether "Mrs. Wilson had any right to mention Daisy's name." Fitzgerald then delivers a description of violence that has since been imitated by countless writers. Rather than drawing out the sensational in a moment of violence, he delivers only the facts. The restraint forces the reader to imagine the details, making the moment both as fast and as brief as it must really have been while simultaneously allowing readers to dwell on the particulars they themselves devise. The prose matches the action: "Making a short deft movement, Tom Buchanan broke her nose with his open hand." The description almost puts one in mind of Hemingway, whose "theory of omission" stated that if a writer leaves out all but the most essential details, a reader will fill in the rest, thus participating in the experience and making it the more powerful. (Though Fitzgerald would not meet Hemingway until the spring of 1925, after he wrote *Gatsby*, he was an admirer of the younger writer and sought him out on arriving in Paris.)

Drunk, Nick leaves the party. The only thing he does

afterward is foggily visit McKee to look at photographs. The names suggest a kind of order and resonance: "Beauty and the Beast" might be Daisy and Tom; "Loneliness" might be Myrtle, might be any of the characters in their refined isolation; "Old Grocery Horse," might be an image from the valley; "Brook'n Bridge" might be the conduit between Manhattan and the valley. The end of Chapter Two and its violence, insights, and suggestions weighs on Nick's knowledge of Tom's mistress, more rumors regarding his neighbor, and his own drunken performance. It is a preamble to the excess, longing, and violence to come.

Chapter Three
The chapter begins with one of the more famous passages of the book: the first description of Gatsby's Friday night parties. In it, Fitzgerald summarizes a list of delights and actions that go into the making of a Gatsby event, the particulars meant some fine day to lure Daisy Buchanan to his home. As Matthew Bruccoli, in particular, and many others have pointed out, the passage highlights one of Fitzgerald's tendencies as a writer, and one of his celebrated talents: that of constructing and reeling off lists that both reveal the specifics of a scene as well as suggest character and motion to events.

In this case, the list serves to highlight the magical quality of the parties and how they first impressed Nick and the many other partygoers. The sentences mix numerous poetic qualities: assonance and alliteration, simile and metaphor: "In his blue gardens men and girls came and went like moths among the whisperings and the champagne and the stars." As well, the unusual word pairings are also at work: turkeys are "bewitched to a dark gold," motor boats "slit the water," the hors-d'oeuvre are "glistening," the orchestra plays "yellow cocktail music," and so on. And in a careful display of commentary on the youthful and callow quality of many newly rich attending Gatsby's ostentatious parties, and on the link between men of means and flappers, Nick notes how the bar is stocked with "cordials so long forgotten that most of his female guests were too young to know one from another."

Fitzgerald builds the scene to a frenzy: "The lights grow brighter as the earth lurches away from the sun ... laughter is easier minute by minute, spilled with prodigality." The flappers are "wanderers, confident girls who weave here and there among the stouter and more stable" until "suddenly one of these gypsies, in trembling opal, seizes a cocktail out of the air, dumps it down for courage, and ... dances out alone on the canvas platform." At this display, Nick tells the reader in understatement, "The party has begun." The concluding understatement technique occurs as well in Chapter Four, after another list about Gatsby's parties.

A "girl" breaks open the party. Much of the criticism of *The Great Gatsby* considers the roles and portrayals of women in the book. Much of the action of the novel leading to strange or unruly behavior by men is instigated—actively or passively—by women. Gatsby's desire and fortune-craving are inspired by Daisy. Daisy also charms Nick before repelling him and changing his understanding of the world he has encountered. Myrtle and Daisy both work on Tom in different ways, and George Wilson is more attached to his wife, and more vulnerable to her loss, than he thinks, while Tom emerges as protective of Daisy. That's not to say that women in the novel are not complete characters with actions and motivations all their own; Daisy is certainly complicated and full of a variety of purposes. But Fitzgerald has a history of writing about women who inspire in men extreme behaviors. It is thus no surprise that a party of Gatsby's cannot truly begin until a young woman has, in her zeal, become a spectacle.

Nick arrives at the first party at the behest of Gatsby; an invitation arrives via Gatsby's butler (dressed, notably, in blue). Nick attends, dressed in white, the color of the Buchanans and their ilk. After all the celebration of the party dressings and the girl emerging as the kick-off for festivities, the first thing Nick notices is commerce: "young Englishmen ... all well dressed, all looking a little hungry, and all talking in low, earnest voices to solid and prosperous Americans." The women are young, impetuous, boozy, and vital; the men are solid, sober, hungry, reserved, scheming.

Nick feels out of place, and is about to "get roaring drunk from sheer embarrassment," when Jordan Baker finds him. As he begins to speak with her, two young women (in yellow dresses) approach her, star-struck by her celebrity as a golfer. As they talk, Nick learns that one of them had torn her (blue) dress at a previous party, and that Gatsby had sent her a new one (the cost is $265, another instance of detail revealing much about character, status, and the like). One of the girls notes, importantly, that "There's something funny about a fellow that'll do a thing like that ... He doesn't want any trouble with *any*body." One of the girls then says, "Somebody told me they thought he killed a man once."

Another breaks in with the rumor that he was a spy, another that he had grown up in Germany, and so on. The speculation causes others to lean in, to try to hear more. Gatsby is the source of much discussion, causing Nick to observe: "It was testimony to the romantic speculation he inspired that there were whispers about him from those who had found little that it was necessary to whisper about in this world."

After bolting from dinner, Nick and Jordan go to look for Gatsby, as Jordan senses Nick's discomfort at not yet having met the host. In the library, however, they find an older man in spectacles, drunk, looking over some of the books, crying that the library actually held things of substance—an important comment given the ethereality of the parties, the women, the conversations, the rumors. In some ways, situated far into the house, concealed from most and away from the parties, the library symbolizes the kernel of substance at the heart of the mythical Gatsby. The old man, later, crashes a car to conclude the chapter, a foreshadowing of the disaster to come.

Nick and Jordan leave the library, the site of substance, to return to the party, where the dancing consisted of "old men pushing young girls backward in eternal graceless circles." Nick watches the scene of "superior couples holding each other tortuously" as he sits at a table, drinking champagne until "the scene had changed before [his] eyes into something significant, elemental, and profound. At that moment, he meets Gatsby for the first time, when the host recognizes him from the military—providing the first tangible and seemingly true information about Gatsby.

Only after a brief conversation does Nick realize the man he speaks to is Gatsby. When he does, his observations sharpen, contradict, and paint Gatsby in a memorable paragraph wherein the man is forcefully revealed as cultivating his own persona:

> He smiled understandingly—much more than understandingly. It was one of those rare smiles with a quality of eternal reassurance in it, that you may come across four or five times in life. It faced—or seemed to face—the whole external world for an instant, and then concentrated on *you* with an irresistible prejudice in your favor. It understood you just as far as you wanted to be understood, believed in you as you would like to believe in yourself, and assured you that it had precisely the impression of you that, at your best, you hoped to convey. Precisely at that point it vanished—and I was looking at an elegant young roughneck, a year or two over thirty, whose elaborate formality of speech just missed being absurd. Some time before he introduced himself I'd got a strong impression that he was picking his words with care.

Note the use of "seemed," "believed," "impression," "convey," "picking"—words all in support of creating an image. Note the final line, about Gatsby's picking his words carefully. Nick is aware of Gatsby's ability to charm (not unlike Daisy's) as well as his careful work in making "elegant" and elaborately formal someone who was once a "roughneck," and perhaps still is. Thus, even when Nick experiences Gatsby in person, after all the innuendo and rumor, he is unsure if the man he is meeting is genuine or just another invention, similar to the rumors. Of course, Gatsby *is* an invention; the reader simply does not yet know this to be true. Fitzgerald has carefully layered the first impression such that the evidence and suspicion are present in the very language, so that the reader's impressions of Gatsby have the same uneasy quality as Nick's.

Gatsby leaves to take a call from Chicago, a town most famous at the time for corruption: Upton Sinclair's book *The Jungle*, published nineteen years before *The Great Gatsby*, had exposed the horrible state of the meat-packing industry. Theodore Dreiser's *Sister Carrie*, published in 1900 and set in Chicago, painted the city unflatteringly and had been deemed obscene by the U.S. government. Most recently, Prohibition had led to the rise of gang activities most famously connected to Al Capone. Given the context of conjecture regarding Gatsby's past, his taking a call from Chicago creates an atmosphere of suspicion.

On Gatsby's departure, Nick reveals to Jordan that he had expected Gatsby "would be a florid and corpulent person in his middle years." The unspoken suggestion was that Gatsby was too young, a bit too dashing, to have really worked for the massive fortune he had attained. He had not inherited it, that anyone knew, so how did he come about it? Jordan reveals another rumor, that he had attended Oxford, and she doesn't believe it.

As the orchestra launches into another bombastic work (with the pretentious title, *The Jazz History of the World*), Nick watches Gatsby not only maintain rectitude in the face of his clamorous party, but also actually become more careful as everyone around him descends into stumbling incoherence. Gatsby is utterly separate from all of it in ways that will mirror Nick's own isolation as it develops later. As he observes his host's near exclusion from his own party, Jordan is called away, as Gatsby wishes to talk with her alone.

The party begins to falter—a famous singer descends into a sobbing despondency, husbands and wives start fighting, girls hiss at their paramours, women are "lifted, kicking, into the night" as their dates take them home at the late hour. Nick waits in the hall, near the library, from which Gatsby and Jordan soon emerge. Notably, Gatsby had taken her to the library—the spot of substance—to ask her a favor, to be revealed in the next chapter. Nick apologizes for not seeking the host earlier, and Gatsby brushes it off.

As Nick leaves, he sees an accident. The "owl-eyed" man from the library had crashed his "coupé," and there is much animated discussion from the crowd about how the accident could have been much worse. The moment is clear foreshadowing, and a hint of the consequences to the mad fanfare of the night, and possibly of the era, though Fitzgerald was seldom one to moralize overtly in his serious fiction. But Nick, as a character and a narrator, certainly possessed the capacity for judgment. While he withholds it at the moment, he has told readers that he looks back on the events with some scorn and disdain. The realization that comes to him as he views the wreck is the first step toward his developing that scorn: "A sudden emptiness seemed to flow now from the windows and the great doors, endowing with complete isolation the figure of the host, who stood on the porch, his hand up in a formal gesture of farewell." Cast against the chaos of the street, the gesture becomes absurd, haunting, foreboding.

Following the party, Nick pauses the story—as if feeling the need to set the drama of the parties and betrayals into a context of his life. He tells of how the events themselves aroused little interest until later, and that his days were, instead, filled with work, with time, and with the city itself and its romantic possibilities. Even so, his enjoyment was tinged with isolation: "At the enchanted metropolitan twilight I felt a haunting loneliness sometimes, and felt it in others—poor young clerks who loitered in front of windows waiting until it was time for a solitary restaurant dinner—young clerks in the dusk, wasting the most poignant moments of night and life." The passage reveals a conflict in Nick (that was actually also a conflict in Fitzgerald): he does not want to be among the lost masses, the inhibitors of valleys of ashes, people lost in the industrial vastness of what Eliot termed a "waste land." On the other hand, he did not want the tragic, false, and cheap magic of the Gatsby partygoers. The frustration becomes increasingly important later in the book.

Nick is also, he tells us, taken with Jordan Baker, and seeing quite a bit of her. He feels toward her a "sort of tender curiosity," something different from love. He details how, like Daisy, Jordan is about appearances—only instead of Daisy's buoyancy, Jordan prefers a mask of "boredom" that covers her "incurably dishonest" nature.

By this point in the novel, the only people Nick has met who are forthright are also on the fringe: the owl-eyed man and the "Finn" who cleans his house. And he reasserts his own honesty, but not until after one last bit of foreshadowing of the accident to come. After noting that Jordan is a bad driver, they have the following exchange:

> "Either you ought to be more careful, or you oughtn't to drive at all."
> "I am careful."
> "No, you're not."
> "Well, other people are," she said lightly.
> "What's that got to do with it?"
> "They'll keep out of my way," she insisted. "It takes two to make an accident."
> "Suppose you meet somebody just as careless as yourself."
> "I hope I never will," she answered. "I hate careless people. That's why I like you."

Of course, everyone she knows is careless—precisely the thing Nick notices about the East Egg residents as well as the partygoers, and the thing for which he develops intense animosity by the novel's end. Such carelessness, as he sees it, leads to avoidable tragedy, recrimination, and the dissolution of lives and fortunes.

Chapter Four
Returning his attention to his neighbor, Nick begins the next chapter with a sardonic assessment of the Sundays at Gatsby's, when "the world and its mistress" would return to "twinkle hilariously" on the lawn for cocktails and a last delight before the work week. The hilarity and over-the-top nature of Nick's statement yield then to the list, the famous recital of partygoers that has attracted the attention of many critics. In its riotous

specifics, the list tells readers of the parties' ability to attract the ambitious, the curious, the newly rich, and the socially ungracious—the literary puns are extensive. In all, though, the list has not a few betrayals, maimings, strange events, and murders contained within, as well as the reiteration of young women as status objects and ciphers for wealth and influence. The details form an exultation that ends with the understatement of "All these people came to Gatsby's house in the summer."

Nick's understatement suggests how deeply he has become enmeshed in the fabric of Fifth Avenue and East and West Egg—how he has come to see not spectacle, but a kind of regularity to events and people suggesting a skewed understanding of the status quo. He has forgotten his own Midwestern roots, though readers also understand he will return to them by the story's end (and, indeed, he writes of Gatsby only after having returned there). The last sentence also underscores the disconnect of the privileged and the aspiring from the situation of most people in the country—in the valley of ashes particularly.

The overdone quality of everything related to Gatsby and West Egg is further reinforced in the next section, wherein Gatsby arrives to take Nick to lunch, driving his elaborate car. Don Seiders discusses much of the symbolism related to objects in the novel, and cars in particular. It is important to note that the car's overblown quality signifies Gatsby's wealth as well as his conspicuous lack of the understated mores that characterize Daisy and Tom Buchanan.

The invitation and trip to lunch is but the latest "urgent invitation" of Gatsby to Nick. By this point in the novel, Gatsby realizes Nick's relation to Daisy, and readers realize later that Gatsby has worked to rapidly develop a friendship with his neighbor, such that he could exploit it to hasten his "accidental" reunion with Daisy. At the same time, Nick observes Gatsby, attempting to reconcile what he knows and can discern from Gatsby with the rumors swirling about him. For instance, when Gatsby arrives in the car, Nick notes his posture, balancing on the running board of the car, "with that resourcefulness of movement that is so peculiarly American—that comes, I suppose, with the absence of lifting work or rigid sitting in youth and, even more, with the formless grace of our nervous, sporadic games." In other words, Gatsby has the bearing one would expect of a member of the leisure class.

Aware of both Nick's observation and the whisperings that surround him, Gatsby divulges his history—a very calculated story—to Nick as they drive. Gatsby claims he descended from wealth in the "Middle West," and when Nick asks where, exactly, he came from, Gatsby answers, "San Francisco," revealing a lack of knowledge about geography (making the Oxford claim seem the more specious) as well as the likely fabrication of his past. Gatsby moves on, talks in "threadbare" phrases such that Nick sees only "a turbaned 'character' leaking sawdust at every pore." He "swallows" or "chokes on" the phrase "educated at Oxford," and his entire bearing as well as his glance seem sidelong to Nick. However, just as Nick is suppressing "incredulous laughter," Gatsby begins to talk about the war, shows Nick pictures from Oxford, reveals accurate details about parts of the world until Nick tells how his "incredulity was submerged in fascination now; it was like skimming hastily through a dozen magazines."

Clearly, Gatsby has arranged the confessional moment. He had with him his medal for military service, his picture from Oxford, and the occasion of a long drive. He also has a favor to ask of Nick, but only through Jordan—thus Gatsby has utilized a romantic relationship (as he perceived it) for his own romantic ends. Gatsby has arranged things well, if a bit hastily and clumsily. Nick has learned enough of his past that appears demonstrably true, and likes Gatsby well enough on top of it, that he is primed for a favor. In one last show—calculated or not—Gatsby is nearly pulled over by a police officer on a motorcycle. But when Gatsby flashes his Christmas card from the commissioner, the cop lets him go, the Gatsby image firmly established.

Immediately afterward, Nick and Gatsby cross over the "great bridge" into Manhattan, and the description of their entry blazes with motion and white, from the sunlight's "flicker upon the moving cars" to the city's skyline of "white heaps and sugar lumps." Nick says, "The city seen from the Queensboro Bridge is always the city seen for the first time, in its first wild promise of all the mystery and the beauty in the world." The Queensboro Bridge enters Manhattan from the east, right at the bottom of Central Park, where some of the most famous architectural landmarks in Manhattan are visible. Thus, the momentary insight and revelation of the Gatsby history end in the panorama of what is to Nick the financial and cultural capital of the world. As they cross, however, a "dead man" passes them in an ornate funeral procession, and the deceased's friends "looked out ... with the tragic eyes and short upper lips of southeastern Europe" and Nick was "glad that the sight of Gatsby's splendid car was included in their somber holiday."

This inclusion does a few things worth noting. First, it juxtaposes the rarefied position of Gatsby, Nick, and the Manhattan skyline with death, the end for everyone, from which Gatsby flees, in a way. It is an early hint of the tragic imagery and consequences of excess waiting in later chapters. As well, it shows the further distancing of Nick from what he might term the "plebeian." Finally, as the paragraph goes on, it draws further distinction between Nick and Gatsby and the other people of various races and ethnicities.

Critics have recently devoted much consideration to the portrayal of race and ethnic differences in Fitzgerald's work, and in *The Great Gatsby* particularly. Nick's statement, "Anything can happen now that we've slid over this bridge," suggests a slackening or loosening of the rules governing places like Fifth Avenue and East Egg, or it could suggest something darker, related to the mixing of individuals so forcefully lamented by Tom Buchanan in the novel's opening chapter. In the very next scene, Wolfsheim's Jewish identity is depicted in ways most contemporary readers would find offensive to some degree. Given the themes of class privilege and racial preference present to varying degrees in *The Great Gatsby* and Fitzgerald's other works, as well as some of the contradictory behavior of Fitzgerald himself with regard to racial and ethnic sensitivity during his lifetime, recent scholarship has had much with which to work.

As for Wolfsheim's contribution to the plot, the scene does two things. It reveals to Nick that Gatsby deals with shady characters. Not only does Wolfsheim wear cufflinks made of human molars, he helped fix the 1919 World Series. Wolfsheim also lends more credibility—to the extent a gangster can—to Gatsby's history, reiterating the "Oggsford" connection. At the end of the scene, Tom Buchanan happens to catch sight of Nick. Tom tells Nick how Daisy is "furious" because he hasn't called. When Nick introduces Gatsby to "Mr. Buchanan," Gatsby is clearly uncomfortable, and then he quickly disappears. Immediately afterward, Nick segues into the story behind Gatsby and Daisy.

The story paints Daisy, once again, in white. Gatsby meets her before he goes to war, and does so when the houses in Daisy's neighborhood are festooned with "red, white, and blue banners." Fitzgerald wanted the resonance of American identity in the scene, and the idyllic meeting of the two under such circumstances was so powerful that the novelist wanted, for a short time, to name the novel *Under the Red, White, and Blue*. The tale also paints Gatsby again as the man possessing the ability to look at people and charm them. Jordan tells the story, as she grew up with Daisy in Louisville, and was best friends with her. It is Jordan who assures Nick that Gatsby looked at Daisy "in a way that every young girl wants to be looked at at some time, and because it seemed romantic" to her she has "remembered the incident ever since." Tragically, to hear Jordan tell it, Gatsby leaves, disappears for four years, during which Daisy has her debut and soon becomes engaged to Tom Buchanan from Chicago. Jordan notes that he gave Daisy a "string of pearls valued at over three hundred and fifty thousand dollars."

Daisy, however, is reluctant. Jordan finds her drunk and despondent just before the bridal dinner, clutching a letter and a bottle of wine, having thrown her pearls into the trash. As Jordan and Daisy's mother work to sober her up, she refuses to let go of the letter, even taking it into the cold bath they make her take. The letter disintegrates "like snow" and no one ever learns what was on it. The prose and the mode of the tale leave the powerful suggestion that Gatsby had written the letter. Daisy marries, discovers Tom is a philanderer (in an anecdote that also operates as yet another foreshadowing of the novel's climactic events), and gives birth to her daughter, and while she and Tom travel, Jordan characterizes Daisy as enduring, not drinking much, not developing a reputation, despite their wild crowd. All seems settled. Then, however, she hears the name Gatsby on the night that Jordan stays at the Buchanans, and it troubles Daisy enough that she wakes Jordan to ask more about him.

Later, while riding in a carriage through Central Park, Nick also learns that Gatsby moved to the mansion on West Egg so he could be near Daisy. In modern terms, given his behavior, his reading of Chicago newspapers, and his elaborate scheming, one might consider Gatsby a stalker. But even in the more forgiving context of social interaction among the reckless inhabitants of West Egg, his behavior gives a little pause. Fitzgerald constructed a character whose romantic understanding of the world runs smack into realism, cynicism, and disillusionment—much the way the author's sense of the romantic drove him to write realist novels dealing with the disconnect between romantic and pragmatic world views. In short, as James E. Miller, Jr., once noted, Gatsby displays the dangers of idealizing an unworthy or even sinister object. Nick feels the conflict of those dangers, borne of admiring Gatsby's unfaltering spirit while disapproving of his methods and scorning his acquisitiveness. But Nick feels the same conflict elsewhere: enjoying the charms of the people he meets while feeling repulsed by their cynical and reckless behavior.

As a result, he grows more attracted to Jordan, whom he refers to as a "clean, hard, limited person, who dealt in universal skepticism." He hears a phrase "beat" in his ears, a philosophical realization borne of his experiences, and it reveals what he has come to understand: "There are only the pursued, the pursuing, the busy, and the tired." As Jordan tells Nick how Gatsby wants him to invite Daisy to tea, Nick considers how he fits into the four groups in the phrase, and determines:

Unlike Gatsby and Tom Buchanan, I had no girl whose disembodied face floated along the dark cornices and blinding signs, and so I drew up the girl beside me, tightening my arms. Her wan, scornful mouth smiled, and so I drew her up again closer, this time to my face.

The moment suggests a number of interpretations: is Jordan so different, so much a mix of realism and scarcely concealed need that Nick finds her "truer" than others? Or, is he caught in the moment of romance and heedlessly loving what is closest at hand? Milton R. Stern suggested, in *The Novels of F. Scott Fitzgerald* (1970), that the Jordan-Nick relationship paralleled the Gatsby-Daisy relationship: Nick is lured into hope and puts aside obvious hurdles through denial. In Nick's case, the obvious hurdle is the fact that Jordan, at base, is fundamentally dishonest, a cheat at her profession, a cynic whose pallid expression belies the scorn she feels for others, and a deserter in times of trouble (as she does in Chapter Seven, after the accident). Stern further points out that her bad driving, referred to throughout the novel, is a symptom of her underlying poor moral character, and that which Nick rejects. While Gatsby himself is a man made from crime, he emerges from the novel a sympathetic character, showing how Fitzgerald, through Nick, values the dream and the capacity for hope more than just about anything else.

Chapter Five
By this point, Fitzgerald has laid the foundations for the climactic events of the novel to unfold. In this chapter Daisy and Gatsby will meet, precipitating events that will result in the shattering of Gatsby's dreams and the bringing about of his untimely death. These events will also galvanize Nick's disdain for the life of the rich—and by extension demonstrate Fitzgerald's own indictment of American culture—and thrust Tom and Daisy Buchanan back into the spiral of meaninglessness and recrimination to which their lives had descended.

The chapter opens with fire imagery applied to Gatsby's house, lit up at two in the morning. He was, he tells Nick, looking into the rooms, surveying his possessions or judging the effect of the place. Nick comments that the house looked like "the World's Fair," raising evocations of the Chicago fair of 1899, another connection with the city that, until the rise of Wall Street, stood for progress as well as the less savory corruptions and muckraking journalists of the previous era. The connection, applied again to Gatsby, is still not flattering.

Nick tells Gatsby he will invite Daisy to tea the following day, but Gatsby makes him wait another day, so that he can hire someone to cut the grass in Nick's yard. Later, Gatsby will insist on flowers and baked goods, working hard to engineer the moment to specifications he has long imagined. Gatsby continues to work on sweetening the incentives for Nick, even offering to help him make "a nice bit of money," to which Nick demurs, despite Gatsby's assurances that Nick wouldn't have to work with Wolfsheim. Nick's pause ensures his removal from everyone as the narrative moves on.

Gatsby and Daisy each have their character on full display in the scene. When Nick phones Daisy about the tea, and asks her to come alone, she misinterprets willfully and flirts almost automatically. Gatsby shows up for the event visibly bothered and dressed in a gaudy mix of silver, gold, and white. He is even a bit off his act, almost forgetting to drop his trademark "old sport" affectation while he talks with Nick.

When Daisy arrives, Fitzgerald again announces her with distinctive prose style:

> Under the dripping bare lilac-trees a large open car was coming up the drive. It stopped. Daisy's face, tipped sideways beneath a three-cornered lavender hat, looked out at me with a bright ecstatic smile.
> "Is this absolutely where you live, my dearest one?"
> The exhilarating ripple of her voice was a wild tonic in the rain. I had to follow the sound of it for a moment, up and down, with my ear alone, before any dash of words came through. A damp streak of hair lay like a dash of

blue paint across her cheek, and her hand was wet with glistening drops as I took it to help her from the car.

While the typical unusual pairings are present ("wild tonic") as well as the density of description, the passage is also distinct due to its presenting Daisy, for the first time, not in imagery related to air, but to water. As well, the tone has changed; no longer white, she arrives in lavender, blue, and lilac. It is a different Daisy that arrives at West Egg, to Nick's home.

She continues to flirt as well, asking Nick, "Are you in love with me ... or why did I have to come alone?" Immediately after she is inside, Gatsby knocks, drenched with rain, or, given the imagery of Daisy's arrival, thoughts of her. He glares at Nick, marches into the home, and while the image seems comical, Nick reminds the reader, "It wasn't a bit funny."

The strain of the moment comes through in Gatsby's posture, in the pauses and delays in conversation, in the ridiculous conversation about the clock Gatsby nearly upends. Nick tries gamely to host, but as Gatsby gets "himself into a shadow" and Nick and Daisy endure his unhappy eyes, Nick soon decides to leave. Fraught with nerves, Gatsby follows him, declares the meeting a mistake, and Nick talks him back into the room, ultimately, by pointing out that Gatsby, the instigator of all of it, was being rude by leaving Daisy alone in the other room.

Fitzgerald's narrator then amplifies the moment's tension by leaving the discussion and directly not talking about it. As earlier noted, such omission can often cause readers a more visceral reaction to the work by imagining, themselves, what transpires. In this case, however, readers have the added tension of not knowing, really, what either person might say. While the conversation happens, Nick muses on the house Gatsby acquired, and the previous owner's similar misunderstanding of what wealth did and did not allow. In noting it, Nick makes one outright statement regarding American culture—a rare such move for the book which, itself, is an implicit indictment of American culture: "Americans, while occasionally willing to be serfs, have always been obstinate about being peasantry."

The rain ceases, the grocer arrives at Gatsby's, the house opens, and soon Nick returns inside, to find them both moved by whatever has transpired. Daisy is teary, Gatsby exultant. Daisy is referring to Gatsby as "Jay," and at Gatsby's suggestion that she see his house, the reason for his hours spent room-gazing become apparent: he wanted to see how they would look to Daisy.

As he asks Nick how the place looks, he divulges that it took him only three years to earn the money to buy it, and in his boast reveals more about his past than he realizes. Nick calls him on it, says, "I thought you inherited your money." His answers, automatic and snippy, arouse yet more curiosity in Nick, which results in more cagey behavior from Gatsby. Before it can worsen, Daisy reappears and the trio tours the grounds and the house, Daisy all the while admiring.

While Gatsby's home is ornate and expensive, the colors gold, lavender, rose, and more reveal its "gaudy" outsider status—there is no white. The silhouette is described as "feudal," primitive, and gauche, and the rooms are distinctly wrong in the age of Modernism and Art Deco. As Gatsby surveys with Daisy, he watches her the entire time, as though he "revalued everything in his house according to the measure of response it drew from her well-loved eyes." The house, once still and from which he isolated himself during parties, comes alive as it finds its purpose, and Gatsby's appreciation for it changes.

As he is stunned by "wonder at her presence," finally comfortable enough with her response and confident with the way things are going, they enter his bedroom, the "simplest room of all," perhaps since no one else ever sees it. Like the library, it has special status different from the rest of the house, something of truth about it. But once there, he opens his patent cabinets and reveals his shirts, "piled like bricks," a relevant description, given how they (and other possessions) have built the man.

The shirts are all colors but white, and as he tosses them to the bed, Daisy begins "to cry stormily." She cries because the shirts are so beautiful, and because she has not seen their like.

Tom, presumably, buys white shirts only, muted suits, the understated style befitting old wealth. And Daisy, married to a man long since bored with his wealth and those things it enables him to acquire, seldom sees ostentatious and beautiful objects. Moreover, Daisy herself is a possession of which Tom has grown tired. She is fine, lacking color and verve, nearly porcelain, and Tom views her as such, in stark contrast to Myrtle Wilson. Wilson's energy is not something he purchases, and she is not refined in the ways Daisy is. For as much as Daisy is enamored of wealth and the lifestyle to which she is chained with golden shackles, so to speak, she does not benefit from the ability to acquire in the way, being new to wealth, she would like. Hers is not a world of zeal, but a world of scornful sophistication, a world of white.

The moment of triumph cannot last. In the very next scene, the rain returns, and the mist shrouds the Buchanan home— something Gatsby points out to Daisy. As Gatsby does so, Nick watches his neighbor mull over the importance of what he has just said:

> Possibly it had occurred to him that the colossal significance of that light had now just vanished forever. Compared to the great distance that had separated him from Daisy it had seemed very near to her, almost touching her. It had seemed as close as a star to the moon. Now it was again a green light on a dock. His count of enchanted objects had diminished by one.

The last sentence above signals the beginning of the end. Gatsby has attained the momentary attention of his lost love, and has achieved the goal to which he has devoted five years of his life. But he also did not yet have it; Daisy would go home at the end of the day. As well, the realization would come soon that the love he hoped to recreate could never be the same, if it had indeed ever really been as he had imagined (a possibility for which the text leaves ample interpretive room).

After that moment, Nick notices the photograph of Dan

Cody, setting up the further development of Gatsby's past set to happen in the next chapter. As Nick does so, Daisy looks, too, and notes how Gatsby never told her anything about the yachting. As she protests, he tries to draw her attention to newspaper clippings of her that he has collected, when the phone rings. The conversation suggests something shady, hinting at a past that will trouble Gatsby's attempts at rejoining with her. When the conversation ends, Gatsby exclaims that Klipspringer, the boarder in his home, will play the piano for them all.

As Gatsby and Daisy sit on a couch in a darkened corner, Klipspringer plays music entirely inappropriate to the tensions in the room. Nick notes the dusk outside, the return of West-Eggers from New York, the "hour of a profound human change" when "excitement was generating on the air." At that point, Klipspringer sings how "the rich get richer and the poor get—children." The conflation of misread intent, a tense reunion, the shattering of expectations, and the energy of threat and storm in the air affect Nick as well as Gatsby. Even though the two of them were "possessed by intense life" in the tumult of the moment, Nick notes:

There must have been moments even that afternoon when Daisy tumbled short of his dreams—not through her own fault, but because of the colossal vitality of his illusion. It had gone beyond her, beyond everything. He had thrown himself into it with a creative passion, adding to it all the time, decking it out with every bright feather that drifted his way. No amount of freshness can challenge what a man will store up in his ghostly heart.

He also guesses that it is Daisy's voice that holds Gatsby with its "deathless song." When Nick leaves, alone again, outside of their collusion, his isolation is again increased and reaffirmed. The overwhelmingly uncertain and negative cast to the events of the afternoon ends the chapter with a kind of dread—a dread that will not be satisfied by events until Chapter Seven.

Chapter Six

To delay the inevitable confrontation and further develop the mysterious man at the heart of the novel, Fitzgerald makes the decision to change pace at the beginning of Chapter Six and deal a bit with the development of Jimmy Gatz into Jay Gatsby. When a reporter seeks out Gatsby for a comment regarding controversial happenings on Wall Street, it is because his name was dropped in the office and, as he was the source of speculative legends, the reporter took initiative on his day off and sought a comment.

Nick points out that for some reason or another Gatsby took satisfaction in the legends. Insomuch as they might have been heard by Daisy, it's easy to see why Gatsby would enjoy a little notoriety. It would help with the attraction factor.

But Nick reports more of the rationale for Gatz's change, reasons that predated his meeting Daisy Fay. In another moment revealing some of the novel's thematic concerns with social class, Nick tells how Gatz's parents were "shiftless and unsuccessful farm people" and that their young son "never really accepted them as his parents at all." Gatz's vision of himself, Nick relates, was "Platonic." The word refers most commonly to an idea expressed in Plato's "Allegory of the Cave," in which Plato relates his philosophy that all worldly manifestations are but versions of an ideal, the perfection of which can never be expressed in actual existence, only approached. For Jimmy Gatz, "Jay Gatsby" is the manifestation of an ideal projected by a seventeen-year-old boy desperate to be glamorous and from another place and time. As Nick points out, in Gatsby's focus, he never allowed the vision to mature. The lack of maturity in his cultivated identity is exactly what Tom Buchanan and others like him sense and reject in Gatsby.

Gatsby's past is, according to a number of critics, Fitzgerald's spin on the typical Horatio Alger tale. Readers of *The Great Gatsby* would have been, on the whole, more familiar with such tales than would today's readers. A very popular nineteenth-century author, Horatio Alger published a string of similar tales in which young men of modest means would, through their own stout-heartedness, ingenuity, and American pluck, rise above and prevail over their native situations to become captains of industry, leaders of men, and altogether virtuous American types. Gatz's tale, with its protagonist who "knew women early," who lived "beating his way along the south shore of Lake Superior" essentially as a mercenary sailor, who "lived naturally through the half-fierce, half lazy work of bracing days," was the typical Horatio Alger protagonist in far grittier circumstances. His imagination foresees "a universe of ineffable gaudiness," all the pomp of wealth. For Gatsby, coming from nothing, the promise of wealth is the promise to *have* everything. Tom Buchanan might well have noted that the promise of wealth is the ability to depend on nothing. While Nick supposes Gatsby had some sense of the unreality of his dreams ("a promise that the rock of the world was founded securely on a fairy's wing"), Gatsby also had enough faith in hope, and enough instinct, to put himself near opportunity and to seize it—like an Alger hero.

However, Gatsby's story turns when he meets Dan Cody. A former miner from what was still an American wilderness, Cody had vast stores of wealth, and was thus the target of "an infinite number of women" bent on separating "him from his money." Looking for a suitable mate for his ill-advised seaward voyage in a yacht, Cody trolled the coast for help. On meeting Gatsby, Cody took him on, seeing in him ambition and judgment, and made the young man, for all intents and purposes, his ward.

While Gatsby had earned his claim on a partial inheritance from Cody, and Cody had made provisions for it, a woman (note the role, yet again, of another woman in the novel) made use of legal maneuvering to deny Jay Gatsby his legacy of $25,000. He was left only, as Nick says, "with his singularly appropriate education; the vague contour of Jay Gatsby had filled out to the substantiality of a man."

Nick points out that Gatsby only tells him of the past much later. (Chapter Eight reveals that Gatsby tells the story in the very early morning following the car accident that kills Myrtle Wilson.) Nick still feels a loyalty to Gatsby, the only person from the summer for whom he still holds any affection, and so notes that he tells the story to dispel the rumors that became worse after the scandalous death. But he tells the story, he says, to let the reader know about the past and its impact, the true sad story of the man. He also tells it because, as he says, there was a pause after the dreadful afternoon spent with Gatsby and Daisy. He doesn't say why, but Nick's character and tone imply the awkwardness as well as the feeling of having been used might have played a part in the break.

The story also colors the reader's understanding of the scene immediately following the history, in which Tom Buchanan's small riding party arrives at Gatsby's for a quick drink. Gatsby effuses, and the party greets his enthusiasm with disdain—a fact clear to Nick but not to Gatsby. Gatsby asserts himself toward Tom, mentions he knows Daisy, to which Tom mutters only, "That so?" The man, Sloane, and the "pretty woman," are only mildly more talkative. The woman suggests they attend Gatsby's next party, and it is possible she is joking. Sloane accepts Gatsby's tacit invitation "without gratitude." The entire party believes itself above Gatsby. Gatsby, however, bent on a good showing and, more particularly, driven to see more of Tom, takes their niceties as serious invitations, much to Tom's consternation. Tom says to Nick:

I wonder where in the devil he met Daisy. By God, I may be old-fashioned in my ideas, but women run around too much these days to suit me. They meet all kinds of crazy fish.

The irony, of course, utterly lost on a boor of the magnitude of Tom Buchanan, is that George Wilson might well bemoan the "crazy fish" his own wife met while "running around too much these days." Shortly afterward, in another move signaling low character, the trio leaves, abandoning Gatsby as he is off in the house, preparing to accompany them.

Tom's jealousy has him at Daisy's side the following Saturday as the two attend Gatsby's party, each for the first time. Nick senses "an unpleasantness in the air, a pervading harshness that hadn't been there before," or, more accurately, that his experience had not yet caused him to see. Daisy's eyes are having an effect on the way he sees the party now, just as they had an effect on Gatsby's own sense of his possessions and achievements. As such, Nick muses:

> West Egg [is] a world complete in itself, with its own standards and its own great figures, second to nothing because it had no consciousness of being so, and now I was looking at it again, through Daisy's eyes. It is invariably saddening to look through new eyes at things upon which you have expanded your own powers of adjustment.

Many people have made the mistake of remembering the eyes on the most famous jacket cover of *The Great Gatsby* as the eyes of Dr. Eckleburg when, in fact, they are a woman's eyes, eyes often read as Daisy's. Daisy's gaze changes the way Nick and Gatsby see the world in which they are embroiled, and her face is itself representative of all Gatsby wishes to achieve. The eyes of Eckleburg represent other things—as detailed in the excerpts in this volume's next section. But perspective and its change—whether as a result of class, sex, or a change in character—are major themes of the novel, expressed ever more forcefully in the later chapters of the novel.

The entire sense of being "second to nothing" due to having "no consciousness of being so" is also often seen as a greater criticism of American exceptionalism, the nationalistic sense of absolute superiority and greatness in all things on which American culture writ large periodically asserts. The decade of the twenties is notable for its optimism and sense of manifest and pre-ordained American greatness, a feeling for which the Great Depression was a most horrible comeuppance. Given its overwhelming feel of dread, illusion and tragedy, and its particular focus on American affluent culture as well as the pointlessness of existence in the valley of ashes, *The Great Gatsby* has been read as Fitzgerald's statement of warning, despite his life's paralleling the excess of his novels.

As the party gets under way, Daisy flirts, the behavior now

almost automatic, and Tom glares and scans the room. Tom states that he would "rather look at all these famous people in—in oblivion," while Daisy, on watching a director work to be able to kiss a starlet, declared she found the scene offensive. Nick states that she found it offensive because it was real emotion, and not gesture.

> She was appalled by West Egg, this unprecedented "place" that Broadway had begotten upon a Long Island fishing village—appalled by its raw vigor that chafed under the old euphemisms and by the too obtrusive fate that herded its inhabitants along a short-cut from nothing to nothing. She saw something awful in the very simplicity she failed to understand.

According to Nick (and, thus, Fitzgerald) Daisy and Tom are insulated by wealth and the mores of restraint and gesture. They are cynical and dead to all emotion from their protected spot, far from struggle. They, and others like them, the affluent dressed in white with their pallid faces, having never known struggle and the feelings of agony and triumph, hold nothing but scorn for such extremes. Additionally, Broadway has "begotten" West Egg by allowing a new route for people of average or lowly means to shortcut the access to wealth and, thus, privilege. "Ordinary" people can now attain the province of the elite.

Thus, Tom's jealousy of Gatsby arises more from his feeling violated by a person of a lower station than out of any real concern for his own wife. Of course, Tom does not see how his zeal for Myrtle Wilson is ironic in this setting; his lies to avoid having to marry Myrtle, however, speak to his fear of "mixing" classes.

Daisy's action at the party, however, mixes revulsion and interest, automated flirting as well as a moment of singing which results in her having "tipped out a little of her warm human magic upon the air." The difficulty of her reaction speaks to how she has a little in common with Gatsby; while he has attained wealth through a secondary means (questionable business actions instead of inheritance or lineage), she has attained it through the only slightly more honorable mode of marrying into it. She might well have ended up like Myrtle Wilson, had she bought into Gatsby's early overtures.

As the party winds down, Nick reports that both Daisy and Gatsby are in a state of high agitation. She is worried about what might happen between her and Gatsby. Still uncertain, still torn, Nick says "her glance" revealed a worry over the "romantic possibilities" of those parties, and that "some authentically radiant young girl"—that is, someone not composed of gesture and affectation—"would blot out those five years of unwavering devotion." For Daisy, a woman for whom adoration is most important, such a change (now that she knows of the half-decade mission) would be ruinous. As for Gatsby, his agitation is more anticipation for what, in his mind, *must* happen next: "He wanted nothing less of Daisy than that she should go to Tom and say: 'I never loved you.'"

Nick and Gatsby walk a "desolate path of fruit rinds and discarded favors and crushed flowers," a symbolic treading if ever there was one. At this time, Nick suggests to Gatsby, "You can't repeat the past," to which Gatsby responds, "incredulously. 'Why of course you can!'" Nick imagines Gatsby seeing the full trajectory of his life in that moment, from back when it all began: Daisy's "white face," when he "wed his unutterable visions to her perishable breath." He placed immortal dreams upon something mortal, perishable, changeable, uncertain. The rock of his existence was, he might be learning, sand.

Chapter Seven

The longest chapter by far in *The Great Gatsby*, Chapter Seven is the fruition of Fitzgerald's layers of style and theme as well as particulars of character, events, exposition, and setting. The events lead to the death of Myrtle Wilson, Daisy's abortive betrayal of Tom, Gatsby's ruin, the end of Nick and Jordan's affair, and the beginning of George Wilson's murderous quest.

The foreboding begins immediately. For the first time since

his arrival in West Egg, Gatsby does not throw a party: "the lights failed to go on one Saturday night—and, as obscurely as it had begun, his career as Trimalchio was over." *Trimalchio* was another of the titles Fitzgerald considered for the novel, and a full explanation of Trimalchio's resonance for Gatsby and his role in the novel can be found in *Trimalchio: an Early Version of The Great Gatsby* by James L. West III. Nick notes that the servants are new, and do not seem servants so much as people temporarily assuming the role of servants. The observation suggests more bad dealings in Gatsby's business affairs. Gatsby himself informs Nick that the servants are "some people Wolfsheim wanted to do something for," and that he needed discreet individuals, given that Daisy is now visiting in the afternoons.

Daisy invites Nick to lunch at the Buchanan house, as well as Jordan Baker and Gatsby. The day of the lunch is hot—with actual heat as well as tension. But where Jordan and Daisy repose, it is cool. And, of course, white, with silver, and in motion with "the singing breeze of the fans." Nick and Gatsby arrive as Tom argues on the phone about selling a car, indicating George Wilson is on the other line. When Tom returns from the phone call, Daisy sends him back to make a cold drink. Once Tom leaves, Daisy kisses Gatsby and tells him she loves him.

Jordan reproaches her for it, and Daisy displays a range of emotion in a remarkably short amount of time. Jordan's remark makes Daisy look around "doubtfully," but then Daisy counters, attempts a dance to show she doesn't care a whit for convention, but as her daughter comes into the room, reverts to an overblown affectation of motherly love. The child has a different effect on Gatsby, making real Daisy's bond to Tom in ways that his willful denial could no longer overcome.

As the daughter leaves, Tom reappears with gin rickeys. As they drink, Tom prevails on Gatsby to go outside, to "have a look at the place," asserting himself in the only way he knows. The effect is not what Tom had hoped for; instead, Gatsby points out the location of his own home, "right across from you." Tom's response echoes his earlier, suspicious "That so?"

He says, simply, "So you are." Just as he exercises restraint in his style, home, and bearing, he exercises it in his distaste. Gatsby, being the character he is, and newly schooled in manners, cannot be as subdued. He almost *has* to point out the house, to show Tom what he had long intended.

Back inside, as Daisy lobbies to go to town, Tom continues to attempt his domination of Gatsby through his home. Asserting that he has made stables from his garage, almost no one hears him, other than Nick. The room has become a place where each individual within it has begun to pursue her or his agenda. Then, when Gatsby and Daisy exchange a glance from which Daisy finds it most difficult to disengage, Tom sees and hears that his wife declares she loves Gatsby. At that point, Tom interrupts Daisy and insists they all go to town.

While the women prepare to depart and Tom goes to get whiskey for the trip, Gatsby and Nick have one of the novel's most famous exchanges:

> Gatsby turned to me rigidly:
> "I can't say anything in this house, old sport."
> "She's got an indiscreet voice," I remarked. "It's full of—" I hesitated.
> "Her voice is full of money," he said suddenly.
> That was it. I'd never understood before. It was full of money—that was the inexhaustible charm that rose and fell in it, the jingle of it, the cymbal's song of it.... High in a white palace, the golden girl ...

Daisy's ability to be indiscreet is bought—her charm derives from her wealth freeing her from any real consequence. She can afford to be devil-may-care, flirtatious, and so on, since she is financially insulated and protected from the outcomes of her behavior. Nick's realization of the source of her charm sets yet another brick in the wall building between himself and the Buchanans and all they stand for. Jordan states early in the novel that she cannot abide careless people, yet it is most clearly Nick who has difficulties with the wages of carelessness and the attitudes that go with it. Nick is the one shocked at ruin and consequences.

At the same time, Gatsby realizes the spot into which he has gotten himself. The daughter has made real the depth of marriage that, however ill-conceived, is still powerful. It is also important that Gatsby be the one to notice Daisy's symbolic alliance with money; the girl and the dream are one, "golden." Both are to be acquired.

When Tom returns, he insists on driving Gatsby's car, while Gatsby and Daisy (after some disagreement with Tom) follow together in the coupé. Tom's anger rises once they start off. Tom tells Nick, accusingly, that he is not as dumb as Nick and Jordan must think, and reveals that he has checked on Gatsby's background. As tensions rise and they ride silently for a while, Nick notes Eckleburg's eyes, both reminding the reader of the presence of either a ruinous god or an unblinking conscience over the valley of ashes. It also sets up the need for gas, and the necessary stop at Wilson's.

At Wilson's, Tom lets George mistakenly assume Gatsby's elaborate car to be the one he plans to sell. George is also shifty—he tells Tom he has "wised up to something funny," and that he and Myrtle plan to move west. Tom, stunned, asks about it, and Wilson confesses that his haste has led him to ask about the car.

Early in the scene, George is described as "hollow-eyed" and sick, and Fitzgerald is once again using eye imagery at a moment of tension. Nick observes, "there was no difference between men, in intelligence or race, so profound as the difference between the sick and the well." To Nick, George appears guilty, perhaps not even of sound mind. He looks a wreck, spiritually as well as physically. As Nick turns away from the guilty aspect of the garage proprietor, he sees "over the ashheaps the giant eyes of Doctor T.J. Eckleburg kept their vigil." However, he also mentions other eyes, the third in the scene: those of Myrtle, tragically misreading what she sees.

The scene is rife with misunderstanding: Jordan doesn't understand Tom's reactions, Tom is unclear on Gatsby's background, George has only an inchoate sense of his wife's transgressions or of Tom's transactions, and Myrtle mistakes Jordan for Daisy. In essence, no one except the dispassionate eyes of Eckleburg and the narrator himself is seeing anything with clarity.

As they approach Manhattan, the city is transformed from its earlier sugar heaps to the "spidery girders"—a place Jordan calls "overripe," now that it is too hot, too tense, too similar to the "hot whips of panic" now lashing at Tom. In the city, Daisy has the drunken idea that five rooms and five cool baths would help ease the heat. The idea devolves into "a place to have a mint julep," and they wind up renting a room at the Plaza.

Once in the room, Tom seizes on the first opportunity to light into Gatsby. When Tom accuses Daisy of making the heat worse by "crabbing about it," Gatsby says, "Why not let her alone, old sport?" After an awkward moment, Tom asks, "All this 'old sport' business. Where'd you pick that up?" The question is a clear challenge to what Tom perceives, partly correctly, as Gatsby's invented persona.

The wedding below them causes Daisy to recall her own wedding then, and a series of memories leads Tom to question Gatsby further. The wedding is another thematic reminder of the situation into which Gatsby has insinuated himself. When Tom finally confronts Gatsby directly, asking, "What kind of row are you trying to cause in my house, anyhow?" Daisy steps in to defend Gatsby, asking Tom to have "self-control." Daisy's asking for such is not only ironic, given her role in the affair, but also telling of what she prizes most: the gesture. Tom is guilty of showing emotion and, however boorish and unsympathetic a character he has been made to be, his emotional response is genuine, something for which earlier chapters have established Daisy has considerable disdain.

Tom's comment in return—"I suppose the latest thing is to sit back and let Mr. Nobody from Nowhere make love to your wife"— is also telling, as if it would be preferable to him that Mr. Somebody from Somewhere were to do it instead. In Tom's world, of course, that would make a bit more sense. For both Tom and Daisy, the moment is fraught with challenges to the very different sanctities they each hold.

Gatsby, too, reveals that which he values most. He becomes most animated when he says, thinking to strike a death blow, "Your wife doesn't love you ... she's never loved you. She loves me." For Gatsby, the love of the golden girl, the final attainment after the upward struggle, is the most important thing. He thinks that his saying it will undo Tom and bring Daisy to him. It does not. Tom dismisses him "automatically." As Gatsby makes his case, however, he does cause Tom to defend himself, even through the tactic of owning up to "sprees," with the assertion that he always returns. Daisy tells Tom he's "revolting," but even then, she does not fully capitulate to Gatsby's wish, to tell Tom she never loved him. The one time she does so is with "perceptible reluctance." In the moment when truth matters, she is unsure which gesture will compel her to the next scene. Thus, when her confused honesty finally surfaces, it is the first of many rebukes of Gatsby's dream. She does confess to having loved him— Gatsby's romantic ideal—but the ideal is flawed because in the same breath, she avers that she loved Tom as well. Nick describes the intensity of Gatsby's response: "Gatsby's eyes opened and closed."

Tom sees that the idea is anathema to Gatsby, so he pursues it. When he says, "there're things between Daisy and me that you'll never know, things that neither of us can ever forget," Nick tells: "The words seemed to bite physically into Gatsby." Gatsby takes his last refuge, insisting that Daisy is leaving Tom. Daisy temporarily says she is, "with a visible effort." At that point, Tom reverts to his original tactic, questioning Gatsby's background.

The argument over merit has its base in money, as if wealth, gotten only one way, were the sole permission for actions. Tom's savagery and the novel's portrayal of him suggest to many critics much about Fitzgerald's feeling regarding American culture at the time, particularly among the social elite. But the other idea at work in the entire exchange is the place of the romantic, the dreamer, in such a culture. Daisy's actions in the scene, particularly, have generated much writing, not only about gender roles, but also about Fitzgerald's attitude toward tenets of Romanticism as expressed in the novel. Nick's description of the remainder of the fight suggests some of the novelist's thinking: "But with every word [Daisy] was drawing further and further into herself, so that he gave that up, and only the dead dream fought on as the afternoon slipped away, trying to touch what was no longer tangible, struggling unhappily, undespairingly, toward that lost voice across the room." For Gatsby, the realization is complete: the past is gone. There is no way to recreate that perfect moment.

Tom, "with magnanimous scorn," sends Daisy and Gatsby along home, together, in Gatsby's car. Some have speculated about why Tom decides not to take the car back, especially given the conversation with George and the ability to further embarrass Gatsby, but it is also clear that Tom believes, by savaging Gatsby's "worthiness," he has short-circuited any risk. Once Gatsby and Daisy have left, Nick suddenly realizes it is his birthday. He has turned thirty—adulthood, middle age, and a kind of maturity, suggest themselves, parallel to the worldly maturity he is attaining during the singular summer on West Egg. He notes:

Before me stretched the portentous, menacing road of a new decade.

It was seven o'clock when we got into the coupé with him and started for Long Island. Tom talked incessantly, exulting and laughing, but his voice was as remote from Jordan and me as the foreign clamor on the sidewalk or the tumult of the elevated overhead. Human sympathy has its limits, and we were content to let all their tragic arguments fade with the city lights behind. Thirty—the promise of a decade of loneliness, a thinning list of single men to know, a thinning briefcase of enthusiasm, thinning hair. But there was Jordan beside me, who, unlike Daisy, was too wise ever to carry well-forgotten dreams from age to age. As we passed over the dark bridge her wan face fell lazily against my coat's shoulder and the formidable stroke of thirty died away with the reassuring pressure of her hand.

So we drove on toward death through the cooling twilight.

Nick equates youth with dreams, and age with the loss of hope, of friends, of expectation. The destruction wrought in the room at the Plaza exacerbated that loss. Then, of course, the tragedy made it worse.

Nick's narration changes from a reportorial, experience-based mode to one more expository. The accident is told from great distance, as he circles down toward the terrible moment wherein Daisy struck and killed Myrtle Wilson. Fitzgerald has Nick begin far from the circle of characters, from the vantage point of the eyewitness, Michaelis. He tells how George has locked Myrtle in her room to keep her from fleeing, how George has suspected Myrtle's cavorting with the coffee shop owner, how the newspapers named Gatsby's vehicle "the death car," how Myrtle had demanded that George have the brass to "beat" her, before she ran into the street and, seeing what she thought was Tom, ran out to stop him.

After describing the savagery of the damage wrought on Myrtle, Nick returns to reportorial mode. In the exchanges that follow, Tom learns that Gatsby's car has hit Myrtle. Tom talks with George, to make sure George does not tell police it was his car. As he does so, he is able to maintain his composure and exonerate himself from suspicion. However, his composure is short-lived; once he leaves with Nick and Jordan, Nick sees Tom stricken with tears and rage. Thinking Gatsby had been driving, Tom says, "The God damned coward! ... He didn't even stop his car."

When they arrive at the Buchanans, the house is still a vision of light and movement, despite the darkness and the circumstances. Disgusted with everyone, Nick doesn't go in, and remains outside alone. Since she owes so much of her existence to the Buchanans, Jordan enters the house. As Nick turns to leave, to meet his taxi back to West Egg, he encounters Gatsby lurking in the trees, wearing a ridiculous pink suit. Nick finds everything about Gatsby, as well, "despicable." For Nick, ultimately, a woman has died from carelessness. For the rest, the matters of importance have to do with status and relationships. Gatsby is more concerned with protecting the stupid and selfish actions of Daisy than with the fate of Myrtle. Tom professes loathing for Gatsby more forcefully than any feeling of loss.

Finally, Nick realizes the truth, and why Gatsby has remained: Daisy had been driving when the car hit Myrtle. More importantly to Gatsby, however, he wants to know Tom is not bothering Daisy about "that unpleasantness this afternoon." He tells Nick how "if [Tom] tries any brutality," Daisy will signal for Gatsby. Nick's response is another instance of brilliant understatement in the novel: given all that Nick knows about Tom's real concerns— Myrtle and Gatsby, and certainly not Daisy— as well as how wrongly Gatsby perceives all that is happening, Nick's response could very well be stronger than "He's not thinking about her." His restraint signals not only the muted behavior typical to the elite, it also indicates a fundamental dismissal of Gatsby.

Gatsby's dwindling relevance in Tom and Daisy's lives is reinforced when Nick goes to check on the house. Nick sees Tom and Daisy sitting together, talking intently, Tom's hand atop one of hers, and untouched fried chicken and glasses of ale between them. More than that, however, Nick sees "an unmistakable air of natural intimacy about the picture, and anybody would have said that they were conspiring together."

Gatsby had not penetrated the marriage, such that it was. Nor, really, had Myrtle. For all of the damning of society and accusation contained in the novel, for better or worse, Tom and Daisy were connected. Nick could see it, but Gatsby could not, and would refuse to understand it. He intended to keep vigil, and Nick notes that he will be "watching over nothing." At least, nothing that will be as he thinks it or wants it to be.

Chapter Eight

Gatsby's delusions persist when he arrives home at around four in the morning. As Nick suggests he should leave, Gatsby insists he has to stay to see what Daisy will do, and Nick saw how "he was clutching at some last hope and [Nick] couldn't bear to shake him free." Daisy's behavior is clear, by then, to everyone but Gatsby.

Despite his insistence on believing Daisy will come to him, Gatsby is otherwise humbled, the façade of "Jay Gatsby" having been "broken up like glass against Tom's hard malice." The jig was up, and so with nothing to lose and no face to save, Gatsby tells Nick how it came about. Thus, the importance of the very first few paragraphs of the book: the paragraphs of Chapter One's beginning establish Nick as a confessor for many. It also helps that Nick is the only person who has treated Gatsby consistently to this point in the novel. Even as he tells his story, Gatsby continues to focus on Daisy, telling Nick why she was so powerful a lure.

The passage highlights Gatsby's own feelings of illegitimacy regarding his pursuit of Daisy: while her house enticed with its "ripe mystery," Gatsby knew he was there "by a colossal accident." He was "a penniless young man without a past" who sensed his time amid "gay and radiant activities" was limited, and thus he "took what he could get, ravenously and unscrupulously." Rather than feeling guilty for his subterfuge, having fallen utterly for her charm, Gatsby is "somehow, betrayed"—baited and, once on the hook, left wriggling. Daisy remained in her "rich house, her rich, full life.... [on] her porch bright with the bought luxury of star-shine." She has purchased, however unwittingly, a seat far above him. Gatsby's doom is sealed, finally, when he becomes "overwhelmingly aware of the youth and mystery that wealth imprisons and preserves, of the freshness of many clothes, and of Daisy, gleaming like silver, safe and proud above the hot struggles of the poor." Hot struggles from which Gatsby has only recently found the means to escape, and with those means, pursue a dream made whole in the person of Daisy.

The combination of seeing the "grail" and having about him the wits to achieve it act on Gatsby very powerfully, and he finds, to his surprise, that he loves her. Gatsby tells of the final days before he went to war, how he and Daisy were quite close, and how he worked afterward to regain it, setting in motion his actions for the next few years. Oxford, it turns out, was more an accident than an intention, but he did spend five months there. Daisy remained in rooms "that throbbed incessantly" with a "low, sweet fever" of "pleasant, cheerful snobbery." The world did not change for her, save that Gatsby had left it. When Tom Buchanan arrived and suggested the continuation of her lifestyle, she chose. In another moment of understatement and omission, Nick notes "the letter reached Gatsby while he was still at Oxford."

As dawn breaks, Gatsby still maintains Daisy's preference, through the years, for him. But the story he tells, about knowing how he had lost "the freshest and best" part of the affair, suggests—possibly—his dawning understanding of what had happened. But readers will never know for sure. The gardener approaches and announces he'd like to drain the pool, and Gatsby asks him to wait, as he would like to swim once, since he had not all summer. Nick doesn't want to leave, though he can't figure why, until, as he leaves to head to the city, promising to call, he turns impetuously and shouts, "They're a rotten crowd ... You're worth the whole damn bunch put together." It is the last thing he will say to Gatsby.

Though Nick says he "disapproved of [Gatsby] from beginning to end," he was glad to have complimented him. Readers know from the first chapter that Gatsby, despite his considerable flaws, is valued due to his pursuit of imperishable hope, and that for Nick, that fact redeems him. The final compliment makes it known, and, of course, it also places the final image of Gatsby, in his "rag" of a pink suit, before a background of "white" steps. For a fleeting moment, Gatsby has attained rarefied air.

Later that morning, Nick and Jordan stop talking, their relationship ended. Her only concern, after the tragedy of the night before, is expressed when she says, "You weren't so nice to me last night." To which Nick says, "How could it have mattered then?" Nick might have had even stronger feeling about such a shallow concern, but he does not voice it. Just as they began in a muted way, they end that way as well.

The remainder of the chapter follows the build-up of George Wilson's anger and despair into murderous rage. Michaelis, no longer considered the philanderer, stays with George Wilson through the night, talking with him, trying to soothe him. Michaelis tries to suggest places George can find some comfort or absolution, a church or family, but George has no such connections. In other words, George is a man not connected to the world; rather, he is someone suffering and affected by it, but one who does not contribute or take warmth from it. Hence his position among the ashheaps. As Nick later says of Michaelis: "he was almost sure that Wilson had no friend: there was not enough of him for his wife." Wilson is a man composed of ash and shadow, barely alive.

George does not want Michaelis' comfort. He wants the other man to understand his position. He points out the dog leash, and as Michaelis rationalizes its existence, it occurs to George, "Then he killed her." At the same time, George realizes he can find out who did it, since he knew the car, and that Tom Buchanan knew the owner. As he sits, rocking, not talking any longer with Michaelis, and he sees dawn coming, he begins to plan. At that point, he looks out to the ashheaps and sees how "gray clouds took on fantastic shapes and scurried here and there in the faint dawn wind"—an image that could be literal or could be a stylized symbol for the movements of men like him. Fitzgerald describes the scene:

"I spoke to her," he muttered, after a long silence. "I told her she might fool me but she couldn't fool God. I took her to the window"—with an effort he got up and walked to the rear window and leaned with his face pressed against it—"and I said 'God knows what you've been doing, everything you've been doing. You may fool me, but you can't fool God!'"

Standing behind him, Michaelis saw with a shock that he was looking at the eyes of Dr. T.J. Eckleburg, which had just emerged, pale and enormous, from the dissolving night.

"God sees everything," repeated Wilson.

As Michaelis points out, Wilson's "God" is an advertisement. Beyond that of Wilson and the cadre of characters involved in the tragedy, there is a subtle indictment here of American culture, again. The scene implies Americans' willingness to worship commercialism, as seen through the belief in this advertisement, an ultimately silly and crass attempt to gain customers among the less discerning individuals in the valley of ashes. To be sure, Wilson is also a bit deranged at the moment, and likely had been for some time, but the powerful suggestion—when taken together with other commentary throughout the novel—acts as Fitzgerald's criticism of consumer culture at the time.

For the final death scene of the novel, Nick once again starts at a generous distance from the actual moment, tracking Wilson's steps, describing how George Wilson determined where to go, how he proceeded on foot, and so on. At the same time, Gatsby, while waiting for a phone message from either Nick or Daisy, headed for the pool, to float on a "pneumatic mattress that had amused his guests during the summer." He would use his own indulgent home, finally, for himself. As he does so, floating in the pool, Nick imagines, quite persuasively, that in the clear sunlight, Gatsby might well have had a moment of revelation:

No telephone message arrived ... I have an idea that Gatsby himself didn't believe it would come, and perhaps he no longer cared. If that was true he must have felt that he had lost the old warm world, paid a high price for living too long with a single dream. He must have looked up at an unfamiliar sky through frightening leaves and shivered as he found what a grotesque thing a rose is and how raw the sunlight was upon the scarcely created grass. A new world, material without being real, where poor ghosts, breathing dreams like air, drifted fortuitously about ... like that ashen, fantastic figure gliding toward him through the amorphous trees.

Note how the imagery of nature is no longer "dripping" or "sparkling" or reverberating. It is "frightening" and "harsh," Gatsby is "shivering" and the sunlight is "raw." The ashen figure is, of course, the final realization as well as the figure of George Wilson. It is as close to the moment of murder the novel will come. In the next paragraph, it is the chauffer who hears the shots. When Nick joins the servants to rush to the pool, the water barely moves, and only a "thin red circle in the water" hints at the violence. "A little way off in the grass," Wilson lies dead, having shot himself. As Nick says, "the holocaust was complete."

Chapter Nine

The newspaper coverage is sensational, and the range of Wilson's despair—at cuckolding, at oppression, at his wife's disregard, his conviction regarding God and morality—is "reduced to a man 'deranged by grief.'" Nick becomes Gatsby's only spokesperson, the majority of the man's associates suddenly silent and gone. Of the people involved in the car accident, Tom and Daisy have left for Europe, gone even before the murder had occurred. As Nick looks around the house for anyone to assist with putting affairs in order, he finds only the picture of Dan Cody, a reminder that he is, of course, dealing with a man without a past.

He sends a memo to Wolfsheim, even drives into New York to visit him, and the man demurs, implying that his association with Gatsby would not be good for his "business." At Gatsby's home, a Chicago call comes through, from a man named Slagle, about "business" going bad, and when Nick says he is not Gatsby, the man ends the call. Even Klipspringer, the tenant, wiggles out of attending the funeral despite Nick's badgering. Out of desperation, Nick starts to call revelers, finally stopping when he makes the mistake of calling "one of those who used to sneer most bitterly at Gatsby on the courage of Gatsby's liquor." Nick's contempt builds as he tries to salvage some rightful parting ceremony for Gatsby and discovers, instead, the shallow motivations and callous and fickle character of most of the West Eggers.

It is only after three days that a telegram arrives, telling Nick of the imminent arrival of Henry C. Gatz, Gatsby's father, "a solemn old man, very helpless and dismayed." Mr. Gatz believed fully in his son, at least as Gatsby had sold himself to his father. But the father shows Nick an old copy of *Hopalong Cassidy*, in which young Jimmy Gatz had outlined a schedule for self-improvement. Gatsby had, for his entire life, sought to improve, to rise up from his circumstances, to be the hero of a Horatio Alger tale. He had even, however unwittingly, marked down his schedule on the inside cover of a tale about an American folk hero. The great irony, of course, comes at the end of the section: the funeral for a murdered self-made man to which no one came. At the burial itself, only Owl-Eyes shows up, the man who had admired with surprise the substance of Gatsby's home.

After the funeral, the final pages feature a ruminative Nick Carraway both finishing tasks necessary for the story's denouement and taking stock of the experience. First, he wants to "leave things in order" with Jordan Baker, however "unpleasant" it would have to be. Jordan is her cool and duplicitous self to the end: she tells Nick she is engaged, an obvious lie, and she claims the abrupt dissolution of their romance, by him, to be a new experience. She eventually refers him to the conversation they had about driving a car, in which Jordan had expressed her first distaste for careless people. When she accuses him of being another careless person, he retorts that he is thirty, and thus "five years too old to lie to myself and call it honor." The insult is directed to her, but she says nothing. His statement of being older and wiser is the last thing between them, and his last comment on the matter, complicated by his admission of conflict about it.

With Tom, he is more direct. He doesn't actually *want* to talk with Tom Buchanan, but Tom forces it when they meet accidentally on Fifth Avenue. When Nick nearly spurns him, Tom insists Nick is crazy, goading Nick to ask, "What did you say to Wilson that afternoon?" As Nick figured, Tom told Nick that Gatsby owned the car. Tom is convinced of his rightness in telling Wilson, and goes through his rationalization, complaining of his own suffering through the ordeal. In a show of mercy for Tom or affection for Daisy, Nick withholds the fact that Daisy had been driving the car.

While Nick's mercy doesn't extend to forgiveness or affection of any kind for Tom, it does permit him to understand him. But the understanding is still damning. Because of Tom's skewed sense of entitlement, two people are dead. Daisy was fully complicit in the death of the third. Nick realizes:

> It was all very careless and confused. They were careless people, Tom and Daisy—they smashed up things and creatures and then retreated back into their money or their vast carelessness, or whatever it was that kept them together, and let other people clean up the mess they had made....

The notion of carelessness is reinforced by much of the imagery in Chapter Nine. After Nick concludes that "Eastern life" requires an adaptation to which one is either born or naturally suited, he declares that the problem might have been that none of them—Westerners, all—had been adaptable to it. But then, to Nick, was that bad? He imagines the East

> as a night scene by El Greco: a hundred houses, at once conventional and grotesque, crouching under a sullen, overhanging sky and a lustreless moon. In the foreground four solemn men in dress suits are walking along the sidewalk with a stretcher on which lies a drunken woman in a white evening dress. Her hand, which dangles over the side, sparkles cold with jewels. Gravely the men turn in at a house—the wrong house. But no one knows the woman's name, and no one cares.

The scene is grim, but ultimately of no consequence. If no one cares, nothing is wrong. Yet, to Nick, the great unanswered question in the scene is the fate of the people within it. What happens to the woman? If no one cares, then her life, as well, is nothing of consequence. It is a scene that removes hope and aspiration from existence, rendering the East wholly an endless grim party in which all that matters is the progression itself. Nick acknowledges that the vision is one "distorted beyond my eyes' power of correction," but the events of the novel support the view.

In Nick's vision, what is typical becomes grotesque. As well, his view of Gatsby's house changes. In the end, it is a "huge incoherent failure of a house." A boy writes an obscenity on the white steps. One last guest arrives on a forlorn Saturday, "who had been away at the ends of the earth and didn't know that the party was over." The "big shore places" are closed or closing, and few lights remain. The community is empty, deformed, and tainted. Some critics have noted the spooky prescience of some of the novel's final imagery, given the crash to come four years later.

But as Nick is able to gradually imagine the island in its original form, a "fresh, green breast of a new world," he marvels at humankind's "capacity for wonder," what he feels ultimately was Gatsby's saving grace. Wonder drove Gatsby "a long way to this blue lawn, and his dream must have seemed so close he could hardly fail to grasp it ... Gatsby believed in the green light, the orgiastic future that year by year recedes before us." Our pursuit of it, Nick says, is why "we beat on, boats against the current, borne back ceaselessly into the past."

Critical Views

G. THOMAS TANSELLE AND JACKSON R. BRYER CONSIDER FITZGERALD'S EARLY REPUTATION

When the reviewer for the Boston *Transcript* commented on *The Great Gatsby* in the issue of May 23, 1925, he said that "no critic will attempt, even in the distant future, to estimate Mr. Fitzgerald's work without taking 'The Great Gatsby' into account, even though its author should create many more books." The statement is true: Fitzgerald did create many more books and we do think of *Gatsby* as Fitzgerald's central achievement. But this is not exactly what the reviewer had in mind. He was not advancing any extravagant claims for the excellence of the novel; by saying "*even* in the future," he was merely implying that *Gatsby* represents such an important development in Fitzgerald's career that it will remain historically and biographically important despite the later (and presumably greater) works that will be the full flowering of his talent. At first glance, the statement is one which, read in the light of present-day opinion, may seem farsighted and perspicacious, but which, if read in context and without the hindsight gained from years of Fitzgerald idolatry, is a typical reviewer's comment. The reviewer saw some merit in the book, to be sure, but there is no indication that his remark is anything more (or very much more) than a polite compliment, or that he had singled the book out as one which might possibly be ranked some day among the greatest works of literary art.

The fact is, of course, that it is difficult for a contemporary commentator to detect a future masterpiece—particularly when the work later comes to be thought of as a masterpiece *representative* of its times. The reviewer is likely either to dismiss the work as trivial or to say that no such people as it depicts ever existed. Fitzgerald, now regarded as the historian of the Jazz Age, was frequently criticized during his lifetime for writing about unreal characters or unbelievable situations. A book like *The Great Gatsby*, when it was praised at all, was praised for its style or its insight into American society; it was not given the kind of serious analysis it has received in the last twenty years, with emphasis on its symbolic and mythic elements. The novel may have been compared to works by Edith Wharton, Henry James, and Joseph Conrad, but it was not felt necessary to draw in Goethe, Milton, and Shakespeare, as Lionel Trilling has done. The fact that *The Great Gatsby* has been elevated to such heights serves to emphasize the mildness of the praise (and the vehemence of the criticism) with which it was received. The vicissitudes of the book's reputation form an instructive illustration of the problems involved in literary judgment. Since the book is today read in such a different way from the approach used by the contemporary reviewers (indeed in a way impossible for them), must one conclude that time is a prerequisite for the perspective needed in critical judgments? that a contemporary can never see as much in a work as a later generation can? that it is necessary to get far enough away from the period so that questions of realism in external details do not intrude?

There have been—it goes without saying—admirers of the novel from the beginning. Gertrude Stein wrote to Fitzgerald of the "genuine pleasure" the book brought her; she called it a "good book" and said he was "creating the contemporary world as much as Thackeray did his." T.S. Eliot, after referring to the novel as "charming," "overpowering," and "remarkable," declared it to be "the first step that American fiction has taken since Henry James." Edith Wharton wrote, "let me say at once how much I like Gatsby"; she praised the advance in Fitzgerald's technique and used the word "masterly." And Maxwell Perkins' adjectives were "extraordinary," "magnificent," "brilliant," "unequaled"; he believed Fitzgerald had "every kind of right to be proud of this book" full of "such things as make a man famous" and said to him, "You have plainly mastered the craft."

But the reviewers were not generally so enthusiastic, and several were quite hostile. In the years following the book's publication, there were a few critics who spoke highly of the book from time to time, but the comments on *Gatsby* between

1925 and 1945 can almost be counted on one's fingers, and certainly the significant discussions require no more than the fingers of one hand. Between 1927 and the appearance of *Tender Is the Night* in 1934, there were fewer than ten articles on Fitzgerald, and in these only three important (though very brief) comments on *The Great Gatsby*; between 1934 and Fitzgerald's death in 1940 there were only seven articles, containing a few brief allusions to *Gatsby*, and one discussion in a book; in 1942 and 1943 there was one discussion each year. In 1945, however, with the publication of essays by William Troy and Lionel Trilling, Fitzgerald's stock was beginning to rise, and the Fitzgerald "revival" may be said to have started. It continued at such an accelerated pace that in 1951 John Abbott Clark wrote in the Chicago *Tribune*, "It would seem that all Fitzgerald had broken loose." The story of the changing critical attitudes toward *The Great Gatsby* is a study in the patterns of twentieth-century critical fashions (since the mythic significance of the book was discovered at the same time that the New Criticism was taking over) as well as of the (perhaps) inevitable course of events in literary decisions. It is the success story of how "an inferior work" with an "absurd" and "obviously unimportant" plot became a book that "will be read as long as English literature is read anywhere."

MATTHEW J. BRUCCOLI LOOKS AT FITZGERALD'S MATURATION AS REFLECTED IN THE NOVEL

The Great Gatsby marked an advance in every way over Fitzgerald's previous work. If he could develop so rapidly in the five years since *This Side of Paradise*, if he could write so brilliantly before he was thirty, his promise seemed boundless. Instead of addressing the reader, as he had done in *The Beautiful and Damned*, Fitzgerald utilized the resources of style to convey the meanings of *The Great Gatsby*. The values of the story are enhanced through imagery as detail is used with poetic effect. Thus the description of the Buchanans' house reveals how Fitzgerald's images stimulate the senses: "The lawn started at the beach and ran toward the front door for a quarter of a mile, jumping over sundials and brick walks and burning gardens—finally when it reached the house drifting up the side in bright vines as though from the momentum of its run."[187] In his richest prose there is an impression of movement; here the lawn runs, jumps, and drifts. Again and again, sentences are made memorable by a single word—often a color word, as in "now the orchestra is playing yellow cocktail music."[188]

The technique in *Gatsby* is scenic and symbolic. There are scenes and descriptions that have become touchstones of American prose: the first description of Daisy and Jordan, Gatsby's party, Myrtle's apartment, the shirt display, the guest list, Nick's recollection of the Midwest. Within these scenes Fitzgerald endows details with so much suggestiveness that they acquire the symbolic force to extend the meanings of the story. Gatsby's car "was a rich cream color, bright with nickel, swollen here and there in its monstrous length with triumphant hat-boxes and supper-boxes and tool boxes, and terraced with a labyrinth of windshields that mirrored a dozen suns."[189] Its ostentation expresses Gatsby's gorgeous vulgarity. There is something overstated about everything he owns, and Daisy recognizes the fraudulence of his attempt to imitate the style of wealth. His car, which Tom Buchanan calls a "circus wagon," becomes the "death-car."

Jimmy Gatz/Jay Gatsby confuses the values of love with the buying power of money. He is sure that with money he can do anything—even repeat the past. Despite his prodigious faith in money, Gatsby does not know how it works in society and cannot comprehend the arrogance of the rich who have been rich for generations. As a novelist of manners Fitzgerald was fascinated by the data of class stratification, which he perceived from a privileged outsider's angle. In *The Great Gatsby* social commentary is achieved by economy of means as detail is made to serve the double function of documentation and connotation. The 595-word guest list for Gatsby's parties provides an incremental litany of the second-rate people who used Gatsby's house for an amusement park:

Clarence Endive was from East Egg, as I remember. He came only once, in white knickerbockers, and had a fight with a bum named Etty in the garden. From farther out on the Island came the Cheadles and the O.R.P. Schraeders, and the Stonewall Jackson Abrams of Georgia, and the Fishguards and the Ripley Snells. Snell was there three days before he went to the penitentiary, so drunk out on the gravel drive that Mrs. Ulysses Swett's automobile ran over his right hand. The Dancies came, too, and S.B. Whitebait, who was well over sixty, and Maurice A. Flink, and the Hammerheads, and Beluga the tobacco importer, and Beluga's girls.

The inventory ends with Nick's understated summation: "All these people came to Gatsby's house in the summer."[190]

This famous catalog is the most brilliant expression of Fitzgerald's list-making habit. He compiled chronological lists of girls, football players, songs, and even of the snubs he had suffered. One of his major resources as a social historian was his ability to make details evoke the moods, the sensations, and the rhythms associated with a specific time and place. Fitzgerald referred to the "hauntedness" in *The Great Gatsby*.[191] He was haunted by lost time and borrowed time.

Much of the endurance of *The Great Gatsby* results from its investigation of the American Dream as Fitzgerald enlarged a Horatio Alger story, into a meditation on the New World myth. He was profoundly moved by the innocence and generosity he perceived in American history—what he would refer to as "a willingness of the heart."[192] Gatsby becomes an archetypal figure who betrays and is betrayed by the promises of America. The reverberating meanings of the fable have never been depleted.

The greatest advance of *The Great Gatsby* over his previous novels is structural. Fitzgerald's narrative control solved the problem of making the mysterious—almost preposterous— Jay Gatsby convincing by letting the truth about him emerge gradually during the course of the novel. Employing a method he learned from reading Joseph Conrad, Fitzgerald constructed Nick Carraway as the partially involved narrator who is reluctantly compelled to judgment. Everything that happens in the novel is filtered through Nick's perceptions, thereby combining the effect of first-person immediacy with authorial perspective. As Carraway remarks, "I was within and without, simultaneously enchanted and repelled by the inexhaustible variety of life."[193] This sense of perspective became one of the distinguishing qualities of Fitzgerald's finest fiction.

Notes

The letters *PUL* designate material in the Princeton University Library, but the several collections of Fitzgerald material have not been identified

187. To Ober, received 26 January 1925. Lilly Library. Ibid. p. 74. For the recollections of H.N. Swanson, editor of *College Humor*, see *Sprinkled with ruby dust* (New York: Warner, 1989).
188. Fitzgerald to Mackenzie, March 1924. University of Texas.
189. PUL.
190. PUL.
191. PUL. *Life in Letters*, p. 98.
192. PUL.
193. PUL.

DAN SEITERS ON IMAGERY AND SYMBOLISM IN *THE GREAT GATSBY*

In his third novel, Fitzgerald continues the practice of using the car to characterize. As Malcolm Cowley points out, the

characters are visibly represented by the cars they drive; Nick has a conservative old Dodge, the Buchanans, too rich for ostentation, have an "easy-going blue coupé," while Gatsby's car is a "rich cream color, bright with triumphant hat-boxes and supper-boxes and tool-boxes, and terraced with a labyrinth of windshields that mirrored a dozen suns"—it is West Egg on wheels.[6]

Gatsby's car is an adolescent's dream, the very vehicle for one who formed his ideals as a teenager and never questioned them again. Gatsby is not sufficiently creative to choose a truly unique machine, so he selects a copy of the gaudy dream car spun from the lowest common denominator of intelligence and imagination. Such a car is exactly what an artist might fashion if he were third-rate specifically because he has plagiarized from the common American dream; because he has seen no need for originality; because he has failed to distinguish between romance and reality. Just as Gatsby—part the shadowy gangster who made millions, part the man who could remain faithful to an ideal love for five years—is an odd mixture of pragmatist and romantic, so his car blends colors representing both traits. It is a rich cream color, a combination of the white of the dream and the yellow of money, of reality in a narrow sense. After Myrtle Wilson's death, a witness to the accident describes the car as just plain yellow, which, as color imagery unfolds, becomes purely and simply corruption. White, the color of the dream, has been removed from the mixture.[7] Only the corruption, the foul dust, remains of Gatsby's dream after that hot day in New York. Thus the car becomes one external symbol of Gatsby, his mind, and what happens to his dream.

Even minor characters absorb traits from the vehicles associated with them. Myrtle, who meets Tom on a train and rides to their trysting place in a cab, must depend on others for transportation. With a single brushstroke—one of these taxi rides—Fitzgerald sketches Myrtle: she "let four taxicabs drive away before she selected a new one, lavender-colored with gray upholstery."[8] This choice, worthy of Gatsby, coincides perfectly with the conduct of a woman who would ask, vulgarly cute, whether the dog is a "boy or a girl" (p. 28), who would display McKee's inept photographs on her walls, and who would have "several old copies of *Town Tattle* ... on the table together with a copy of *Simon Called Peter*, and some of the small scandal magazines of Broadway" (p. 29).[9]

Jordan Baker, too, is characterized by her association with cars.[10] Through her handling and driving of them, she reveals herself as a careless person. Nick does not recall the story that she cheated during a golf tournament until she leaves a "borrowed car out in the rain with the top down, and then lied about it" (p. 58). As for her driving, "she passed so close to some workmen that our fender flicked a button on one man's coat" (p. 59). As Nick says, she is a "rotten driver" fully capable of causing a fatal accident if ever she meets someone as careless as herself (p. 59). She smashes things, as do most careless people. The pattern is plain; recklessness behind the wheel (at first humorous in the Owl Eyes scene) deepens to near tragic proportions when it claims the lives of the Wilsons and Gatsby. Neither Nick nor the reader can trust a careless driver. Perhaps even Nick is careless. He does not deny it when Jordan accuses him of being a bad driver. The essential point, however, is that Nick has become considerably more human. No longer the man to make an extravagant claim to honesty, he does not try to defend himself against the charge of careless driving.

Always a characterizing device in *The Great Gatsby*, the car soon develops into a symbol of death. Fitzgerald begins to establish this pattern at the end of Gatsby's party. As the mass of cars leave,

> a dozen headlights illuminated a bizarre and tumultuous scene. In the ditch beside the road, right side up, but violently shorn of one wheel, rested a new coupé.... The sharp jut of a wall accounted for the detachment of the wheel, which was now getting considerable attention from a half dozen curious chauffeurs. However, as they left their cars blocking the road, a harsh, discordant dun from those in the rear had been audible for some time and added to the already violent confusion of the scene. (p. 54)

Carelessness plus cars equal chaos, and although the scene with Owl Eyes—who correctly protests that he knows little about driving and that he was not even trying to drive—is a highlight of humor in the novel, it suggests the possibility of an accident, even a fatality, if a car is placed in the hands of a careless person. This scene is designed to establish the pattern, to prepare the reader for Myrtle's death.

Tom's first experiment with infidelity continues the pattern of careless drivers leading careless lives and reinforces the image of the amputated wheel:

> Tom ran into a wagon on the Ventura road one night, and ripped a front wheel off his car. The girl with him got into the papers, too, because her arm was broken—she was one of the chamber maids in the Santa Barbara hotel. (p. 78)

This second accident adds another element to the symbol. Not only is the possibility of injury or death linked with careless drivers, but infidelity suddenly becomes part of the pattern.

Even here, though, where automobile imagery increasingly symbolizes death, Nick finds taxis a part of the very breath and music of New York:

> When the dark lanes of the Forties were lined five deep with throbbing taxicabs, for the theater district, I felt a sinking in my heart. Forms leaned together in the taxis as they waited, and voices sang, and there was laughter from unheard jokes.... Imagining that I, too, was hurrying toward gayety and sharing their intimate excitement, I wished them well. (p. 58)

Cars, in addition to dealing death, have the more normal function of carrying people to excitement, or to other destinations. Only the driver defines the car.

Viewing automobile imagery from a different perspective, it is significant that Wilson should deal in cars on the edge of the valley of ashes. Like the automobile, he gradually becomes both symbol and instrument of death. As Nick points out, "the only car visible [in Wilson's lot] was the dust-covered wreck of a Ford which crouched in a dim corner" (p. 25). The valley of ashes is the valley of death where everything is dead or dying.

To make sure the reader catches the symbolic significance of the automobile, Fitzgerald, in one master stroke, associates both cars and water with death. As Nick rides with Gatsby over the Queensboro Bridge, they meet a funeral procession: Nick is glad that "the sight of Gatsby's splendid car was included in [the mourners'] somber holiday" (p. 69). To draw attention to this funeral procession and to its importance in the fabric of the novel, Fitzgerald introduces it with the singular, somewhat bizarre phrase: "A dead man passed us in a hearse heaped with blooms ..." (p. 69).[11]

With everything set up to create expectations of disaster whenever a car appears, the accident that kills Myrtle seems inevitable, not the very strange coincidence it really is. Image patterns have made it possible for Fitzgerald to use an unlikely series of events and to make them seem natural. He has led us carefully to the moment when Myrtle lies dead, one breast amputated like the amputated front wheels in earlier scenes.

Temporarily shaken by the loss of his mistress—even though he has just regained his wife—Tom soon recovers and reverts to type. Leaving Myrtle dead in ashes, Tom "drove slowly until we were beyond the bend—then his foot came down hard, and the coupé raced along through the night" (p. 142). Where caution is seemly, Tom pretends to practice it, but away from the public eye, he speeds up, becomes again the fast driver who broke a girl's arm and sheared off the wheel of his car in an earlier accident. This violent event fails to alter Tom; the pattern of carelessness will continue, and Tom will drive on, harming but unharmed.

To cap off the automobile symbolism, Fitzgerald makes all cars become the death car to Michaelis, who spends the night watching Wilson. Whenever a car goes "roaring up the road outside it sounded to him like the car that hadn't stopped a few hours before" (p. 157). And it is symbolically right that the car, even though it has served its purpose in killing Myrtle, should continue to be an image of death. With Myrtle dead, two still remain to die: Wilson and Gatsby. Gatsby's car, symbol of death, of a tarnished dream, leads them all to the grave.

(...)

One first notes that *The Great Gatsby* is built around East Egg, West Egg, and the Valley of Ashes, all of which are characterized in terms of light.[16] A fourth setting, New York, appears less vividly in terms of light, although a harsh sun often gleams there. The preponderance of light imagery establishes *The Great Gatsby* as a "novel about seeing and misseeing."[17] Few characters see clearly. Nick, proclaiming himself honesty's model, sees himself but dimly. Only Owl Eyes dons enormous spectacles to correct his vision:

> Despite his imperfection as a seer (like the other guests, he is drunk), this man is able to look through the facade of Gatsby and all he stands for, and, just as important, he is able to see that there is substance behind the facade.[18]

Owl Eyes views Gatsby *only* from the outside, yet he makes the most telling pronouncement—"The poor son of a bitch" (p. 176). He sees Gatsby as a human being, a man deserving decent burial. Nick sees more, enough to speak a volume, but Owl Eyes cuts quickly to the essence, the humanity.

In a novel where everyone more or less has an opportunity to see, total darkness is rare. Darkness dots play one important role, however; when Gatsby returns home after his all-night vigil at Daisy's window, he and Nick spend the black morning in Gatsby's house: "We pushed aside curtains that were like pavilions, and felt over innumerable feet of dark wall for electric light switches" (p. 147). Apparently they find no light switches because Nick says, "throwing open the French windows of the drawing-room, we sat smoking out into the darkness" (p. 147). Clearly, this is ritual; on this dark night, Nick and Gatsby form a human bond, and Gatsby, for the first time, talks unreservedly about himself. In light—sun, moon, artificial—they form no such friendship. Like King Lear, who sees only after enduring the black night of madness, like Gloucester, who understands only after Cornwell hops his eyes to dead jelly, like Oedipus, who comprehends only after he has gouged out his own eyes, Gatsby and Nick can see one another only in darkness. Perhaps their relationship could not survive the light of day; a better conclusion, considering Fitzgerald's penchant for ironically twisting symbols, is that darkness offers a more realistic picture than light does. Gatsby must become himself because the dark hides his gorgeous suit, his magnificent house, his fabulous car. Gatsby stands as if naked in the dark, and he comes off pretty well. Without his absurd trappings, he is enough of a human being to force the fanatically cautious Nick into a human commitment, something no one else has done.

Just as Nick and Gatsby wait together in darkness on the night of Myrtle's death, Michaelis and George Wilson maintain a vigil in the "dull light" of the garage. At dawn they snap off the light that all through the night has been bombarded by beetles. Wilson looks out over the valley of ashes, not upon the dew and stirring birds as did Nick and Gatsby, but upon the dead eyes of T.J. Eckleburg. Astonished, Michaelis watches as Wilson reveals that he worships Eckleburg as a god. The contrast between the blue-gray dawn of the wasteland and the gold-turning dawn of West Egg is genuine this time, not just apparent. Both Nick and Wilson make commitments in that dawn—Nick to another human being, to life, and Wilson to a gaudy graven image, to death. His commitment is natural in a place where even dawn is described as twilight (p. 160).

Moonlight, which often pierces the night, is a more prevalent image than total darkness in *The Great Gatsby*.[19] The moon in earlier novels symbolized romance; it shed a light that made palatable the harshest realities. Not here, though. The moon becomes the sinister light of nightmare, although it is innocent enough in the beginning of the novel. On the way home from the Buchanans' in chapter 1, for example, Nick notes the brightness of the summer night and the red gas pumps in pools of light in front of the stations. On this night, which teems with life beneath moonlight, Nick sees Gatsby "standing with his hands in his pockets regarding the silver pepper of the stars" (p. 21).[20] Or so Nick thinks. Gatsby sees no stars—natural if romantic lights—but worships the artificial green light at the end of Daisy's dock.

During Gatsby's first party, the moon enhances the

atmosphere of unreality. As evening blurs into morning and the moon rises, Nick finds "floating in the sound … a triangle of silver scales, trembling a little to the stiff, tinny drip of the banjoes on the lawn" (p. 47). Here even nature—in the form of the moon—cooperates to stagelight the production which is Gatsby's party.[21] Nick suggests that Gatsby's power is such that he can dispense "starlight to casual moths" (p. 80).

Moonlight at this point still epitomizes romance. The birth of Jay Gatsby and simultaneous departure of James Gatz occurs under a fantastic moon image. A dream is born; Nick describes the labor pains that bring forth romance:

A universe of ineffable gaudiness spun itself out in his brain while the clock ticked on the washstand and the moon soaked with wet light his tangled clothes upon the floor. (pp. 99–100)

A romantic adolescent gives birth to a dream. That dream never grows, never changes.

Gatsby's dream, however, suffers a blow in the moonlight when Daisy disapproves of the party. The death of Myrtle then sends it reeling, and suddenly the moon is no longer the fabric from which dreams are spun. The moon becomes associated with the grotesque after Myrtle's death: Tom, Nick, and Jordan return from New York, "the Buchanans' house floated suddenly toward us through the rustling trees" (p. 142). Tom becomes callous, decisive in the moonlight: "As we walked across the moonlight gravel to the porch he disposed of the situation in a few brisk phrases" (p. 143). But Gatsby still dreams, stands in moonlight with his pink suit glowing against the dark shrubbery in the background. Whether or not any vestiges of sacrament cling to his vigil, he mans the watch. Moonlight for Gatsby still connotes romance, even intrigue, and Nick leaves him standing in the moonlight, "watching over nothing" (p. 146).

Although he is amazed at Gatsby's belief that he can recapture the moonlit nights with the Daisy of five years past, Nick, too, sets up a romantic image of the West, an image he would recapture. When he leaves the East, which has become an El Greco nightmare under a "lustreless moon," he seeks his Christmas-vacation idealization of the West. He recalls a time when

> we pulled out into the winter night and the real snow, our snow, began to stretch out beside us and tinkle against the windows, and the dim lights of small Wisconsin stations moved by, a sharp wild bract; came suddenly into the air.... That's my Middle West—not the wheat or the prairies or the lost Swede towns, but the thrilling returning trains of my youth, and the streetlamps and sleigh bells in the frosty dark and the shadows of holly wreaths thrown by lighted windows on the snow. (p. 177)

Nick has learned much about human nature. Oddly, he does not know that this winter Arcady no longer exists for him. His chances of returning to it exactly equal the possibilities of Gatsby finding the pure white Daisy of Louisville. This was the Middle West of youth, not of a man five years too old to lie to himself. It exists momentarily for some people, never again for Nick.

Fitzgerald makes one final comment on what happened to Gatsby's dream. The last time Nick sees the "huge incoherent failure of a house," he finds glowing in the moonlight an obscene word scrawled on the steps with a piece of brick (p. 181). Romantic light on obscenity. With the strength and energy to become anything, Gatsby and America plagiarized an adolescent dream. Fascinating, awesome in execution, the product of that false dream remains forever an obscenity.

Nick would wipe away the obscenity, start over with a new dream. The same moon would shine, but the "inessential houses" would melt (p. 182). Knowing the dream impossible, Nick believes in it. With glowing terms of understanding, he describes Gatsby's belief in

> the green light, the orgiastic future that year by year recedes before us. It eluded us then, but that's no

89

matter—tomorrow we will run faster, stretch out our arms farther.... And one fine morning— (p. 182)

The punctuation, the dash comprehends the futility of Nick's hope, as well as the necessity of it. Fitzgerald cannot lie and say the dream might be realized; he dares not proclaim it impossible, and yet he ends the novel with a tone of heavy resignation: "So we beat on, boats against the current, borne back ceaselessly into the past" (p. 182).

The image projected in moonlight, of course, resides in the head of the beholder. Thus moonlight is as man-made as any form of artificial light, and whoever separates the two—artificial light and moonlight—stands on shaky ground. But classifications are always arbitrary, and shaky ground can be profitable. In this case, I think it profitable to discuss artificial light as a separate category.

(...)

If light-dark imagery in *The Great Gatsby* exposes the dream as the product of a third-rate imagination, a thing a bright teenager might create, the dirt-disease-decay imagery shows the dream as tarnished. Both image patterns examine the American dream, the dream that is the subject of *The Great Gatsby*, *Tender is the Night*, and *The Last Tycoon*. In one sense *The Great Gatsby* looks forward to *The Last Tycoon*; it is *The Last Tycoon* inverted. *The Last Tycoon* tells the story of the corruption of those who enter Hollywood. Hollywood functions as dream factory, Stahr as plant manager. He tells the writer, Boxley, "We have to take people's favorite; folklore and dress it up and give it back to them" (p. 105). Stahr decides what that folklore is, dictates what people dream. Despite Stahr's best efforts as artist, corruption riddles his factory of dreams. And Gatsby, the consumer, takes a dream such as Stahr might weave, thinks it his own. The very purity arising from Gatsby's devotion to the dream paradoxically leads to his own corruption. *The Last Tycoon*, then, deals with the corruption of those who manufacture dreams; *The Great Gatsby* explores the plight of the consumer, the man who buys pot metal, reveres it as gold.

References to decay of various sorts appear often enough in *The Great Gatsby* to form a major motif.[25] Decay images fall under three main headings: the valley of ashes; the ravages of humanity against humanity; and moral rot. Each of these categories appears in Nick's famous line containing the essence of dirt-disease-decay imagery in the novel:

> No, Gatsby turned out all right in the end; it is what preyed on Gatsby, what foul dust floated in the wake of his dreams that temporarily closed out my interest in the abortive sorrows and shortwinded elations of men. (p. 2)

The "foul dust" symbolizes the valley of ashes, a vast dead valley that bursts geographical barriers to include both Eggs as well as New York and, by extension, the United States. The valley serves as one huge metaphor symbolic of a land that produces only dust and death. This waste land ranks in sterility with anything in the Eliot poem.[26] While an apparent contrast exists between the waste land and either East or West Egg, the contrast is just that—*apparent*. On West Egg Gatsby produces a "vast meretricious beauty" that serves a purpose for a time, but his empire wilts under the gaze of Daisy. Because his dream was meaningless, hollow, it ends absolutely with Gatsby's death, lies as inert and dead as the valley of ashes. Gatsby leaves no legacy except the story Nick tells.

If the contrast between West Egg and the valley of ashes resembles that of the prairie vs. low, rolling foothills, the contrast between the valley and East Egg should approach that of flatland vs. mountain. Fitzgerald practically forces the comparison by juxtaposing the green light at the end of the first chapter with the waste land images that open chapter 2. Yet East Egg produces nothing that sets it above the dust and death of ashes. The dialogue of East Egg is more sophisticated, but no more original and certainly no nearer any standard of universal truth. Tom's string of polo ponies is of even less practical use than Wilson's aging car. The boredom spawned in each place seems equally intense. And the gray of the ash heaps approaches the dominant color of the Buchanan estate—white.[27]

Foul dust floats from all three places. More clearly than Tom or Gatsby, of course, Wilson sinks into his environment: "A white ashen dust veiled his dark suit and his pale hair as it veiled everything in the vicinity" (p. 26). While Wilson is a part of his environment, he only accepted it, did not create it. Tom and Gatsby are not as guiltless. While both took from others their respective utopian ideas, they at least had a choice over what to plagiarize. Only Wilson, born to exist in the valley of death, had no choice, made no attempt to control.

The waste land pervades both East and West Egg because travelers from either place must cross the valley of death. Nick and Gatsby observe foul dust as they drive into the city:

We passed Port Roosevelt, where there was a glimpse of red-belted ocean-going ships and sped along a cobbled slum lined with dark, undeserted saloons of the faded-gilt nineteen-hundreds. (p. 68)

Fitzgerald highlights this theme of corruption in two ways: first, Gatsby extricates himself from the clutches of a policeman by showing a Christmas card from the commissioner, thus indicating moral corruption from top to bottom, at least in the police department; second, having solved the problem with the law, Nick and Gatsby encounter a problem no one can handle—death. Crossing the Queensboro Bridge, they meet a corpse, the ultimate corruption.[28] Later they meet Meyer Wolfsheim, corruption personified, and he continues the theme of death with his tale of the murder of Rosy Rosenthal.[29]

Appropriately, Myrtle dies in the valley of ashes. Had she not lived in what becomes a major symbol of death and decay, Myrtle might not have sought outside stimuli. Still, the valley of ashes does not kill her; she dies because she met that interloper into the valley of death, Tom Buchanan. Wilson, a soldier in that great army of living dead, dies for the same reason.

The valley provides the setting for the first death, Gatsby's mansion for the next two. After Myrtle dies, Nick and Gatsby spend the night together at what in tabloid parlance will become the death house. Here they seal a friendship, begin to view one another as human beings. Yet the house resembles a tomb: "There was an inexplicable amount of dust everywhere and the rooms were musty...." (p. 147). Gatsby seems to have given up on his house. Already it resembles the valley of ashes, the smoldering remains of dreams.

Leaving Gatsby, Nick boards the train for work. As he passes the valley of ashes, he crosses to the other side of the car to avoid decay and death. He would spurn reminders of mortality. But no one avoids the ash heap. In *The Great Gatsby*, the foul dust of the valley of ashes functions symbolically as a ubiquitous *memento mori*, the symbolic contradiction of Gatsby's belief that a man might wipe clean the corruption of the past and begin anew as innocent as a virgin child.

Juxtaposed with pervasive dirt and decay imagery are references to the ravages of man. Most destructive of all is Tom, who hurts people, wrecks things. He causes pain, is too insensitive to know he does it. The first proof of this is Daisy's bruised finger; Tom does not recall hurting it. Daisy's injury results from one of many accidents, all of which could have been prevented. Tom causes one of many automobile accidents, Daisy another, a more serious one. Carelessness is universal in this novel, but Tom and Daisy, who care less than most people, cause their hog's share of pain through a series of destructive accidents. Tom, who smashes Gatsby's dream as deliberately as he smashes Myrtle Wilson's nose, sometimes is more calculatingly cruel than careless.

Obviously, others besides the Buchanans dispense destruction and decay. Violence lurks forever just below the surface, remains a constant possibility. Tom, booted athlete whole powerful body strains against his riding clothes, finally threatens no more than Gatsby. Because of the amount of energy—and waste—expended to create these parties, a Gatsby festival always presents the danger of unchanneled force: "Every Friday five crates of oranges and lemons arrived from a fruiterer in New York—every Monday these same oranges and lemons left his back door in a pyramid of pulpless halves" (p. 39). Gatsby's parties, and by extension, his way of life, cause decay, burn things up. Efficiency experts would be appalled at the meagerness of the product compared with the energy expended. And damage must be repaired. When a girl rips her gown, Gatsby, to stave off chaos, replaces it with a more expensive one. As Nick observes, after each party someone must repair the "ravages of the night before" (p. 39). Thus Gatsby establishes a cycle: through the week he creates a haven of perfect order only to loose forces of destructive chaos on Saturday night.

The parties end when Gatsby notes Daisy's distaste for his extravagance. He sees the parties through Daisy's eyes. Disconsolate, he walks with Nick: "He broke off and began to walk up and down a desolate path of fruit rinds and discarded favors and crushed flowers" (p. 111). Here he makes the claim that he can repeat the past. He walks in ruins, the ravages of his party, even as he assures Nick that he *can* repeat the past. As Gatsby states his dream, Fitzgerald repeats once more the familiar motif that just below the surface glitter lies ruin. With remarkable economy, Fitzgerald makes clear the dream and makes a symbolic comment on it.

Daisy and Jordan, too, are entangled in corruption imagery. On the Buchanans' wedding day, for example, the heat matches that of the sweltering day in New York when Daisy again renounces Gatsby and reaffirms Tom. At the wedding a man named Biloxi faints, becomes, like Klipspringer, a freeloading boarder. He sponges for three weeks at the Baker house before Jordan's father kicks him out. Baker dies the next day, but Jordan assures Nick that the eviction and death were not connected. Jordan is correct, but the parallel between Daisy's first rejection of Gatsby and affirmation of Tom and that New York scene is deliberate. The common ingredients are intense heat, rejection of Gatsby, and affirmation of Tom followed by death. True to his common practice in *The Great Gatsby*, Fitzgerald tells the same story twice-once humorously, once tragically.

Corruption surrounds Daisy even before the wedding. After

Gatsby leaves for war, Daisy leads a seemingly carefree, innocent life. Yet hints of dirt and decay add ominous hues to the sparkling colors of her social life. At parties feet shuffle the "shining dust" on the dance floor (as Myrtle's feet shuffle "foul dust" of the valley of ashes), and when she falls asleep at dawn, she leaves "the beads and chiffon of an evening dress tangled among dying orchids on the floor beside her bed" (p. 151). Decay images and images of carelessness converge here to indicate that Gatsby's dream is futile from the start. Corruption in Daisy's world is subtle, but definitely present; in Gatsby's world corruption is obvious, but unimportant. Conversely, Daisy's elegance and taste are apparent, but not important; one must search, as Nick does, to ferret out the fine qualities of Gatsby.[30]

Notes

6. "The Romance of Money" from *Three Novels of F. Scott Fitzgerald*, ed. Malcolm Cowley (New York: Charles Scribner's Sons, 1953). See also Vincent Kohler, "Somewhere West of Laramie, On the Road to West Egg: Automobiles, Fillies, and the West in *The Great Gatsby*," *Journal of Popular Culture*, 7 (Summer 1973), 152–58.

7. Daniel J. Schneider, "Color Symbolism in *the Great Gatsby*," *University Review*, 31 (Autumn 1964), 18.

8. F. Scott Fitzgerald, *The Great Gatsby* (1925; rpt. New York: Charles Scribner's Sons, 1960), p. 27. all quotations are from this edition. Page numbers hereafter cited in parentheses.

9. Howard S. Babb, "*the Great Gatsby* and the Grotesque," *Criticism*, 5 (Fall 1963), 339. Babb points out as examples of the grotesque the description of McKee's picture and the "gossip columns which lie side by side with a book concerning religion—all of these contrasts hooting at the vulgarity of Mrs. Wilson."

10. Mathew J. Bruccoli, "A Note on Jordan Baker," *Fitzgerald/Hemmingway Annual* (1970), 232–33. "The name Jordan Baker is contradictory. The Jordan was a sporty car with a romantic image.... The Baker was an electric car, a lady's car—in fact an old lady's car.... This contradiction is appropriate to her character: although she initially seems to share Nick's conservative standards, he is compelled to reject her because of her carelessness." See also Laurence E. MacPhee, "*The Great Gatsby*'s 'Romance of Motoring': Nick Carraway and Jordan Baker," *Modern fiction studies*, 18 (Summer 1972), 208. MacPhee suggests that Fitzgerald derived Jordan Baker's name "from two of the best-known trade names in motoring, the

Jordan "Playboy" and Baker "Fastex" velvet, a luxury upholstery fabric for automobiles." See also Roderick S. Speer, "*The Great Gatsby's* 'Romance of Motoring' and 'The Cruise of the Rolling Junk,'" *Modern Fiction Studies*, 20 (Winter 1974–75), 540–43. Agreeing with MacPhee's thesis that Fitzgerald was both aware of and influenced by romantic automobile advertising when he wrote *The Great Gatsby*, Speer points out that Fitzgerald contributed a serialized article called "The Cruise of the Rolling Junk" to *Motor Magazine*. This article, according to Speer, evinces Fitzgerald's "constant sense of the disappointment always lurking at the fringes of idealism and enthusiasm." This theme "bears directly on that endangered romanticism ... which lies at the heart of *Gatsby*...." (pp. 540–41). Indeed, much of the point of the automobile imagery is that the car, envisioned by the characters as a romantic means of escape, leads in reality down a one-way road toward death.

11. Henry Dan Piper, "The Untrimmed Christmas Tree" in *Fitzgerald's "The Great Gatsby*," ed. Henry Dan Piper (New York: Charles Scribner's Sons, 1970), p. 98. In an earlier version, Gatsby's car was an even more blatant symbol of death than it is here: "In one draft, when Gatsby proudly shows Nick his oversized yellow sports car ('the death car,' as the New York newspapers will later call it after Myrtle's death), Nick is automatically reminded of a hearse."

16. A.E. Elmore, "Color and Cosmos in *The Great Gatsby*," *Sewanee Review*, 78 (Summer 1970), 427.

17. Lehan, *F. Scott Fitzgerald and the Craft of fiction*, p. 120.

18. Dale B.J. Randall, "The 'Seer' and 'Seen' Theme in *Gatsby* and Some of Their Parallels in Eliot and Wright," *Twentieth Century Literature*, 10 (July 1964), 52.

19. Sadao Nishimura, "Symbols and Images in *The Great Gatsby*," *Kyushu American Literature*, 24 (July 1983), 92–95.

20. Schneider, "Color Symbolism in *The Great Gatsby*," 14. Silver symbolizes "both the dream and the reality, since as the color of the romantic stars and moon ... it is clearly associated with the romantic hope and promise that govern Gatsby's life, and as the color of money it is obviously a symbol of corrupt idealism."

21. David R. Weimar, "Lost City: F. Scott Fitzgerald" in his *This City as Metaphor* (New York: Random House, 1966), p. 95. Fitzgerald's attraction for cinema shows up in his prose, in the visual pictures he paints and lights.

25. For an interesting view of depravity in the novel see Keath Fraser, "Another Reading of *The Great Gatsby*," *English Studies in Canada*, 5 (Autumn 1979), 330–43.

26. See John M. Howell, "The *Waste Land* Tradition in the American Novel." (Ph.D. Diss., Department of English, Tulane University, 1963), pp. 9–31; Robert J. Emmitt, "Love, Death, and

Resurrection in *The Great Gatsby*" in *Aeolian Harps: Essays in Literature in Honor of Maurice Browning Cramer*, eds. Donna G. Fricke and Douglas D. Fricke (Bowling Green: Bowling green University Press, 1976); James E. Miller, Jr., "Fitzgerald's *Gatsby*: The World as Ash Heap" in *The Twenties: Fiction, Poetry, Drama*, ed. Warren French (Deland, Fla.: Everet/Edwards, 1975); Letha Audhuy, "'*The Waste Land*': Myth and symbol in *The Great Gatsby*," *Etudes Anglaises*, 33 (1980), 41–54; and Christine M. Bird and Thomas L. McHaney, "*The Great Gatsby* and *The Golden Bough*," *Arizona Quarterly*, 34 (summer 1978), 125–31.

27. Daniel J. Schneider, "Color Symbolism in *The Great Gatsby*," 14. White, the traditional color of purity, is used ironically in the cases of Daisy and Jordan. "Daisy is the white flower—with the golden center," and brass buttons both grace and tarnish her dress. Off-whites, brass and variants of yellow, symbolize money, greed, corruption.

28. Joan S. Korenman, "A View from the (Queensboro) Bridge," *Fitzgerald/Hemingway Annual* (1975), 93–96.

29. Dalton H. Gross, "The Death of Rosy Rosenthal: A Note on Fitzgerald's Use of Background in *The Great Gatsby*," *Notes and Queries*, 23 (January–December 1976), 22–23.

30. See Douglas Taylor, "*The Great Gatsby*: Style and Myth," *The Modern American Novel: Essays in Criticism*, ed. Max Westbrook (New York: Random House, 1966), p. 66:

> The most eloquent irony of the novel is generated by the subtle interplay between, on the one hand, the elegance and charm of Daisy's world as opposed to the cunningness of its inner corruption and, on the other hand, the gaudy elaborateness of Gatsby's efforts to emulate its surface as contrasted with the uncontaminated fineness of his heart.

JOHN F. CALLAHAN ON FITZGERALD'S USE OF AMERICAN ICONOGRAPHY

"In dreams begins responsibility," Yeats recalled at the beginning of one of his volumes, and that is the assertion we must make about Gatsby and the American dream generally. What Gatsby overlooks are the connections between culture and personality. He pursues Daisy without relation to objects, except (an overwhelming exception) as their accumulation is necessary to attain her. He nourishes the fantasy that if one keeps his goal a pure dream, keeps the focus fixed on the same being, nothing else that exists is real or necessary. The logic turns vicious, though, for Gatsby comes more and more to define himself, as best he can—and his best is shoddy and affected—in terms of Daisy's world. Thus when he finally has Daisy again, he desperately and insecurely diverts her from himself to his possessions.

> Look how the sunset catches my house.
> See its period bedrooms.
> Feel all my English shirts.
> Listen to my man, Klipspringer, play my grand piano
> In my Marie Antoinette music room.

He has, during and because of his five-year quest, lost the very contingent "responsiveness" which, one imagines, moved Daisy to him in the first place.

Gatsby's house indeed might as well be a houseboat sailing up and down the Long Island coast, as the rumors contend. "Material without being real," it is both as intangible and as monstrously tangible as his dream. To Gatsby himself it is never real, unless for the moment he wondrously discovers it while showing it to Daisy, who at once sees the house as grotesque and dislocated from its time and place. The house itself? "A factual imitation of some Hôtel de Ville in Normandy" (6). Its brief cycle of ownership has descended from German brewer to dreaming bootlegger. Soon Daisy will find Gatsby himself as irrelevant to her world and culture, to herself, as is his house. So also Gatsby's nightmare began when he wedded his "unutterable visions" to her "perishable breath." We're talking about a particular cultural vision. Even before he met Daisy, Gatsby's focus was upon that "vast, vulgar, and meretricious beauty" of the America over which goddess Daisy presided. Or, to paraphrase a question Nicole Warren will ask late in *Tender Is The Night*: How long can the person, the woman in a Daisy Fay transcend the universals of her culture? In

America, clearly, not very long. An interlude at best. Like the song said:

"In the meantime,
In between time—" (72)

Jay Gatsby was doomed from the start by "just the sort of Jay Gatsby that a seventeen-year-old boy" *in early twentieth-century small-town America* "would be likely to invent" (75). Archetypically American are the materials of his self-creation. True last will and testament seems the biographical document Henry C. Gatz carries East to his son's funeral. On the inside cover of a Hopalong Cassidy comic book read SCHEDULE and as afterthought and afterword: GENERAL RESOLVES. In stark relief issues Gatsby's cultural context before he leaves home for St. Olaf's and thereafter for Dan Cody's service. The SCHEDULE maps out a regimen for every hour of the day. In addition to the Victorian notion of a sane mind in a sound body, there is the implicit encouragement toward ambition, toward the proverbial tradition of American greatness. Worst of all is the proverbial mode which dissociates success from the uses of power.

But young Gatz looked beyond Poor Richard to the master himself in his adolescent determination to "study needed inventions" (131). Yes, between 7:00 and 9:00 P.M. after his self-instruction in "elocution and poise." The GENERAL RESOLVES catalogue those practical-moralistic doses of cultural codliver oil at the root of Franklin's reading of experience (his public reading, that is):

No wasting time at Shafers or (a name, indecipherable)
No more smokeing or chewing
Bath every other day
Read one improving book or magazine per week
Save $5.00 (crossed out) $3.00 per week
Be better to parents (132)

Yet annihilating it all to the sixteen-year-old's imagination is the paper it is written on. No *tabula rasa* this Hopalong Cassidy comic book. Hopalong's white horse and chivalric cowboy adventures utter the fantasy far more graphically and kinetically than do the prosaic Alger-Franklin schedules and resolves. Why shouldn't the young provincial just go and *be* a hero in an America beyond the small town? Hopalong Cassidy has no family either, no continuous identity beyond hat and horse, no responsibilities other than to preserve law and order and keep crime rates low in the Wild West. Who can doubt the inevitability of James Gatz's flight from North Dakota or his creation of Jay Gatsby? Or his switch of filial allegiance from shabby, powerless Henry C. Gatz, like St. Joseph merely a serf in the vineyards, to Dan Cody, patriarch of expansion, man of action and entrepreneur both, a man who could beat the Robber Barons at their game of violent ownership, then draw their jealous admiration at his physical exploits in a Wild West Show? Quite clearly, Fitzgerald means Dan Cody to be a true and historical version of Hopalong Cassidy.

* * *

So in each echelon of the world Nick Carraway enters we find options closed out; in himself because of the failure of sensibility and moral imagination, with the Buchanans because of a lack of "fundamental decencies." In the case of Gatsby the end precedes the beginning because that man fails to plant his identity in subsoil, in earth more responsive to the aesthetic pulse than the twin shoals of an ahistorical yet all too historic false heroic (Alger-Cassidy) *and* a complementary ethic of salvation by accumulation (Franklin-Cody). But what of Carraway himself? He is guilty neither of the amoral cruelty of the Buchanan set—like him or not, he does possess some capacity for relationship—nor of Gatsby's delusion that man can simultaneously ignore and conquer history through a platonic self-creation derived from and modeled on that very same history and culture. What are we, the *we* whom Carraway invokes in his last prophetic sentence, to do with his absolute judgment that aesthetic sensibility has, does, will fail to penetrate history and culture in America? The assumption is so total and so based on a fable whose contexts are so relatively few, it seems we've got to dissociate Fitzgerald from Carraway's vision or, if that distorts the structure and spirit of the novel, then assault Fitzgerald himself with our objections. Somewhere, so goes the latter view, the novelist's own critical judgment and negative capability failed him. Wittingly or unwittingly, Fitzgerald has become the property of his own narrator. This reading has had sufficient exposition.[6] It is, I think, false.

I oppose that interpretation, first, on formal grounds, because of what I believe to be the novel's contingent, contextual principle, and, second, on those biographical grounds most often used contrarily to join Fitzgerald to Carraway in a perceptually Siamese way. It seems to me that, *given the nature and goal of his own quest*, Carraway's conclusions are formally and morally as reasonable as the world he encounters. Even a narrator, after all, can expect to receive no better objects and goals than those he seeks. And Nick Carraway comes East for no other reason than to make his fortune, and thereby himself. True, the stolidity of the Middle West bores him to restlessness. He would have the excitement of a world less charted, more charged. But the metaphor for his identity is economic; he moves from hardware (solid, permanent commodity) to bonds (paper projections of values at a given time contingent upon a certain set of circumstances). Since Carraway would define and establish himself in a mercantile profession (a bond salesman is almost a money-seller, certainly a money-changer), how can he expect the world he discovers to be anything other than a society of accumulation, a world whose only exception, Gatsby, has for his dream object a golden girl, a King Midas's daughter, and who can achieve the dream only if he masters the culture of money? *We*, therefore, have got to stand back from the frame of Carraway's narrative portrait, to see his judgment and prediction as true, inevitable, or universal only given the cultural context he and those in his fable have chosen for their world.

Fitzgerald, I believe, would teach the following lesson: understand and then beware of this context. I say *this* context, because its pervasiveness, its terrific powers of seduction are driven home by its being the only real context. For in *The Great Gatsby* "money is the root of all evil" is refined to read: money is the root of all culture, and, for Carraway, possibly the root of all nature as well.

Note

6. Several critics, among them Leslie Fiedler in *An End to Innocence* (Boston: Beacon Press, 1955), and recently, Richard Lehan, charge Fitzgerald with a failure of critical intelligence in that, they feel, he has not put sufficient distance between his characters'—especially Carraway and Diver's—failures and his own.

MILTON R. STERN ON THE AMERICAN DREAM AND FITZGERALD'S ROMANTIC EXCESSES

It is important here to specify the idea of "the American dream," for the term is used continually, and, unless it is understood clearly, becomes too inclusive and vague a generalization. Except for special (and very natively American) Utopian concepts, the dream is a dream of self rather than community. Whether one confronts the Jeffersonian insistence that the purpose of the state's existence is to guarantee and extend the private and independent liberty of the individual, or one confronts the ideas in *Walden*, "Self Reliance," or "Song of Myself," one reads concepts in which the liberated individual is the measure of value. And in all cases, short story or novel, the dream of Fitzgerald's characters is a dream of self at the lustrous moment of emergence from wanting greatness to being great—Amory's dream. The state of yearning is an expectant present tense dictatorially bound by the future, a repudiation of the present as a state of impatient placelessness in being less than the imagined self, a state of loss to be replaced in the future by being the sublime self whose name everyone knows. It is a dream of self, however clothed, that the history of American expectations—from the conquistadores' greedy vision merged with eighteenth-century ideas of perfectibility and with nineteenth-century Romantic ideologies of the self—developed into an American heritage of the possibility of total transcendence. (Like Fitzgerald, I think that the real history of America, written so far in the literature rather than the history books, is the history of its expectations.) The dream of self is one of absolute liberation from the conditional world of circumstances, from the world of sweat, and of next things, and showing the marks. A secular ecstasy, it is nothing less, in its naive splendor, than what must be called liberation from mortality. Having much in common with American Ahab, Fitzgerald's characters, unlike Ahab's creator, do not read Emerson or Thoreau or Whitman or the continua of thought that channeled into them from the past and out of them into the future; but they do have a sense of the self as a "god in ruins" to be liberated in the future, as a radiant butterfly emerging from the grub, as a "kosmos." In Fitzgerald's mind, the characteristically American idea is an amalgam of feelings, romantic and adolescent emotions, bound up with the historical idea of America as the released new world, and, therefore, with the old promise of the vast Golden West. But Fitzgerald was acutely aware that the idea of the self had been relocated, from the 1880s on, in the shining wealth of the growing, magnetic cities in the East. For Dreiser, Chicago had been the dream city in the making—"It sang, I thought, and I was singing with it"—and for the younger mid-westerner, like Fitzgerald, that dreamworld had already moved further eastward, to New York.

He had long dreamed of "the Far-away East," as he wrote in one of the Basil Duke Lee stories, "Forging Ahead," "the faraway East, that he had loved with a vast nostalgia since he had first read books about great cities. Beyond the dreary railroad stations of Chicago and the night fires of Pittsburgh, back in the old states, something went on that made his heart beat fast with excitement. He was attuned to the vast, breathless bustle of New York, to the metropolitan days and nights that were tense as singing wires. Nothing needed to be imagined there, for it was all the very stuff of romance—life was as vivid and satisfactory as in books and dreams."[5] Fitzgerald knew that the stuff of American wealth was the city sign of the American promise—attainment of the gold was to be attainment of the golden moment. To be rich, for Fitzgerald's characters, and to have the appearances of wealth, were in and of themselves not important. Gatsby was perfectly willing to "turn off" his gaudy house the moment he sees that Daisy disapproves of it. Yet Fitzgerald also knew that for most of American society, the highly imagined Emersonian sense of possibilities had deteriorated to vague and discontented desires for wealth and the commodities and identity of wealth—in short, that the appearances of wealth are at once all there is and are yet empty to the fulfillment of the dream of self beyond wealth. Like Emerson and Thoreau, Fitzgerald knew that in America there had been an enormous displacement of the possibilities of self by the possibilities of wealth, and consequently, that American society, impelled by an undefined heritage of unlimited possibilities, had become a highly mobile, tentative, and obscurely unfulfilled and omnivorous energy directed toward power and luxury, but with no sensitively or clearly defined human ends. Looking about him in the modern moment of the "Younger Generation," even the man of "heightened sensitivity to the promises of life," if he lacks the advantage of an educated understanding of the idea of America, sees only the attractiveness of wealth with which to articulate his unique American response. The energy of the dream is its romantic expectation, but the actuality of the dream is merely its appearances. So the true American, the Columbus of the self, the rare individual within the American mass, is betrayed by his belief in America, by his belief that the appearances are the fulfillment. At this point in his understanding of the American dream, Fitzgerald, in *The Great Gatsby* and *Tender Is the Night*, does the same thing that seventeenth- and eighteenth-century writers had done on both sides of the Atlantic. He used America not as a specific location or nation, but as a metaphor for the deepest longings of the human race, and his "Americans" become Mr. Every Newman. In the specifics of the American locale, however, Fitzgerald saw most Americans, like most men everywhere, desiring merely the substance of respectable wealth, having no imaginative sensibility of anything beyond the identities of money; yet uniquely propelled by a sense of national promise they no longer understand, they remain wistfully perplexed by the feeling that after everything is attained, they are still missing "something." And they drift in an indefinite discontentment, ever seeking "a change." The true believer seems to sum up all the others in his striving for the appearances he believes in, but he stands out from all the rest in his consuming devotion to his goals, the actualization of his certitude of a released and dazzling self to be achieved through the appearances. "The American dream" for Fitzgerald is the continuing story of the rare, true American's total commitment to the idea of America, and the inevitability of his betrayal by what he identifies as the actualization of the ideal. It is in this conflict that Fitzgerald's materials and experience combined to make the composition of *The Great Gatsby*.

(...)

Both Fitzgerald and Gatsby were broken by the extravagance of the emotional expenditure. Both were willing to enter the world of next things, and to try to keep the sweat and marks from showing, old sport, in order to earn the appearances that would permit them to win the dream girl. Gatsby knew full well that when he made Daisy the receptacle of his dreams he would be forever wedded to her. It would henceforth be emotionally and spiritually—if I may say so, *nationally*—insupportable to find the basket broken and shabby after he had put all his East and West Eggs in it. Putting one's self into the American dreamgirl was much more than a genital action for the dreamer. Gatsby "took Daisy one still October night, took her because [in his present identity] he had no real right to touch her hand.... He knew that Daisy was extraordinary, but he didn't realize just how extraordinary a 'nice' girl could be. She vanished into her rich house, her rich full life, leaving Gatsby—nothing. He felt married to her, that was all" (pp. 113–14). The imagined self up there in the transcendent heavens was made manifest in walking flesh, and what flesh can bear the burden? Nick learns what Daisy meant to Gatsby:

> One autumn night [that "still October night" when Gatsby put himself into Daisy] they had been walking down the street when the leaves were falling, and they came to a place where there were no trees and the sidewalk was white with moonlight. They stopped here and turned toward each other. Now it was a cool night with that mysterious excitement in it which comes at the two changes of the year. The quiet lights in the houses were humming out into the darkness and there was a stir and a bustle among the stars. Out of the corner of his eye Gatsby saw that the blocks of the sidewalks really formed a ladder and mounted a secret place above the trees—*he could climb to it if he climbed alone*, and once there he could suck on the pap of life, gulp down the incomparable milk of wonder.
>
> His heart beat faster and faster as Daisy's white face came up to his own. He knew that when he kissed this girl, and *forever wed his unutterable visions to her perishable breath, his mind would never romp again like the mind of God.* So he waited, listening for a moment longer to the tuning fork that had been struck upon a star. Then he kissed her. At his lips' touch she blossomed for him like a flower and the incarnation was complete.

The incarnation of the romping dream of self among the stars (p. 84, italics mine).

Gatsby knew what he knew only because Fitzgerald knew it in the same "unutterable" way. "When I was your age," Scott wrote to his seventeen-year-old daughter,

> I lived with a great dream. The dream grew and I learned how to speak of it and make people listen. Then the

dream divided one day when I decided to marry your mother after all, even though I knew she was spoiled and meant no good to me. I was sorry immediately I had married her but, being patient in those days, made the best of it and got to love her in another way. You came along and for a long time we made quite a lot of happiness out of our lives. But I was a man divided—she wanted me to work too much for *her* [the magazine fiction, the jazzy need for money and a hot-cat life] and not enough for my dream. She realized too late that work was dignity and the only dignity, and tried to atone for it by working herself, but it was too late and she broke and is broken forever.[7]

The letter was unfair, written toward the end of the 1930s, in which he lived through horror after horror. For at the beginning he had plunged as gleefully as Zelda, more wonderingly than she, into the whirl of success. And Zelda paid hideously and pathetically for all the golden girl selfishness and wastefulness and laziness and, above all, irresponsibility, that made her at once so zestful and so much less than Fitzgerald's dream of her. But autobiography is beside the point if it is considered as a set of historical facts. For all the similarities between Fitzgerald's life and Gatsby's, the novel is hardly a point-by-point recapitulation of history. The amazing pool of source materials in Fitzgerald's life for the fiction he wrote, and the countless and obvious parallels between the two, have misled some readers into reading the fiction as autobiography. But those who have reacted against misreadings occasioned by the parallels between the fiction and the biographical facts often react too strongly when they discount considerations of such relationships as a critical mistake. For Fitzgerald's fiction is autobiographical in the deepest sense, a sense that goes beyond facts. It is the autobiography of Fitzgerald's imagination, of his own ecstatic impulses and his imaginative reaction to the exciting American promise of life, whether in St. Paul society, at Princeton, in the expatriate's Europe (Fitzgerald never became Europeanized like Hemingway, never learned the language of the country, remained an unregenerate American and admitted it), or in the ever-beckoning glamour of New York. As Harry Levin has pointed out, the history of the realistic novel shows that fiction" tends toward autobiography.[8] Because the realistic novel attempts to create a sense of "what it's really like," it will necessarily depend upon details that evoke that sense, and nowhere, of course, are those details more clear to an author than in his own memory of the experience out of which that sense arises. In America, the realistic novel has been almost unexceptionably a statement of exposé because of the discrepancy between the romantic New World vision—"the Dream"—and the American details in which that vision is supposed to have been enacted. The American autobiographical memory since the Civil War generally has been stocked with revelations of the extent to which American life falls short of the transcendent vision. A sense of cheat and defeat is particularly characteristic of the fiction of Norris and Dreiser, a school of realism that early struck Fitzgerald as an example of what courageous, serious fiction should be.

Notes

5 *Afternoon of an Author*, ed. Arthur Mizener (London, 1958), p. 47.

7. July 7, 1938, in *The Letters of F. Scott Fitzgerald*, ed. Andrew Turnbull (New York, 1963), p. 32; hereafter referred to as *Letters*.

8. *James Joyce* (New Directions, New York, 1960), p. 41.

JAMES E. MILLER, JR. DISCUSSES STYLISTIC APPROACH TO FIRST PERSON

Fitzgerald's use of the modified first-person enables him to avoid "the large false! face peering around the corner of a character's head."[67] By giving Nick logical connections with the people he is observing, by always making his presence or absence at the events probable, not accidental, and by allowing him several natural sources of information which he may use freely, Fitzgerald achieves a realism impossible to an "omniscient" author or even to a limited third-person point of view: through Nick Carraway, Fitzgerald places the reader in direct touch with the action eliminating himself, as author entirely. What Fitzgerald says of Cecilia, in his notes to *The Last Tycoon*, might well apply to Nick in *The Great Gatsby*: "by making Cecilia, at the moment of her telling the story, an intelligent and observant woman, I shall grant myself the privilege, as Conrad did, of letting her imagine the actions of the characters. Thus, I hope to get the verisimilitude of a first person narrative, combined with a Godlike knowledge of all events that happen to my characters."[68] Fitzgerald could have substituted his own name for Conrad's had he recalled Nick Carraway. *The Great Gatsby* is a minor masterpiece illustrating beautifully Conrad's governing literary intent "to make you *see*."

(...)

Although Gatsby's life is gradually revealed in the novel as an acquaintance's life would probably emerge in real life, there is an artistic order in the disorder. In Nick's pursuit of the "substance of truth" in Gatsby's story, he passes on the information in the order in which he receives it—with one major exception. After briefly recounting Gatsby's days with Dan Cody, he adds: "[Gatsby] told me all this very much later, but I've put it down here with the idea of exploding those first wild rumors about his antecedents, which weren't even faintly true. Moreover he told it to me at a time of confusion, when I had reached the point of believing everything and nothing about him. So I take advantage of this short halt, while Gatsby, so to speak, caught his breath, to clear this set of misconceptions away" (122). Dozens of legends have accumulated around Gatsby: that he is a cousin of Kaiser Wilhelm, that he killed a man once, that he was a German spy, that he was an Oxford man, that he was involved in the "underground pipeline to Canada" (117), and even "that he didn't live in a house at all, but in a boat that looked like a house and was moved secretly up and down the Long Island shore" (117). A desirable amount of bewilderment, confusion, mystery, and suspense is created by these wild stories, but it is necessary that they gradually give way to something really as awe inspiring as the myths themselves, Gatsby's enormously vital illusion. And to understand that illusion, it is necessary to understand its origins, which go far deeper than the love for Daisy. Just as the first half of the novel is devoted to the inflation of the myth of Gatsby to gigantic proportions to give apparent support to the "colossal vitality of his illusion" (116), so the second half gradually deflates this myth through the revelation of the deepness of the roots of Gatsby's dream in the deprivations of his past. The one instance, mid-point in the novel, of Nick's departure from his method of conveying information as it is revealed to him is the book's "fulcrum": the legends must be cleared away so that there might be room for the truth to emerge.

Fitzgerald once remarked of *The Great Gatsby*, "What I cut out of it both physically and emotionally would make another novel."[72] This confession reveals something of the "selective delicacy" with which he dealt with his material. In *The Great Gatsby*, as in neither of his previous novels, the "subject" is unfailingly and remorselessly pursued from beginning to end; yet, contrary to Wells, this novel gives the impression of being more "like life" than either of the other two. Fitzgerald's sympathetic observer, who is narrating the story in retrospect, provides a natural selection, as does the limiting of the action to one summer. But even within these restrictions, Fitzgerald could have indulged in irrelevance or expansiveness. And as a matter of fact, a number of his literary peers criticized *The Great Gatsby* because of its *slightness*. Edith Wharton wrote: "My present quarrel with you is only this: that to make Gatsby really Great, you ought to have given us his early career (not from the cradle—but from his visit to the yacht, if not before) instead of a short resumé of it. That would have situated him, & made his final tragedy a tragedy instead of a 'fait divers' for the morning papers."[73] Fitzgerald wrote to John Peale Bishop about his criticism of *The Great Gatsby*, "It is about the only criticism that the book has had which has been intelligible, save a letter from Mrs. Wharton.... Also you are right about Gatsby being blurred and patchy."[74]

Notes

67. Fitzgerald, "Introduction," *The Great Gatsby*, p. x.

68. Fitzgerald, *The Last Tycoon* (New York: Charles Scribner's Sons, 1941), pp. 139–40.

72. Fitzgerald, "Introduction," *The Great Gatsby*, p. x.

73. Edith Wharton, one of "Three Letters about 'The Great Gatsby,'" *The Crack-Up*, p. 309.

74. Fitzgerald, "Letters to Friends," *The Crack-Up*, p. 271.

JAMES E. MILLER, JR. ON THE MEANING OF THE NOVEL

Shortly after publication of his novel, Fitzgerald wrote to Edmund Wilson, "of all the reviews [of *The Great Gatsby*], even the most enthusiastic, not one had the slightest idea what the book was about."[79] The meaning of the novel is, presumably, neither obvious nor to be comprehended in a simple statement. In one sense, certainly, the theme is the potential tragedy of passionately idealizing an unworthy and even sinister object. But this narrow definition does not suggest the subtlety and complexity of meaning brilliantly achieved by the symbolism, by the imagery, and by the language itself; and it is in these elements that the book is "sparkling with meaning." This phrase recalls Conrad's "magic suggestiveness," and it seems likely that Fitzgerald was attempting to accomplish with language what Conrad had outlined in his preface to *The Nigger of the Narcissus*: "And it is only through complete, unswerving devotion to the perfect blending of form and substance; it is only through an unremitting never-discouraged care for the shape and ring of sentences that an approach can be made to plasticity, to colour, and that the light of magic suggestiveness may be brought to play for an evanescent instant over the commonplace surface of words: of the old, old words, worn thin, defaced by ages of careless usage."[80] Not only has Fitzgerald confessed that he had the words of Conrad's preface fresh in his mind when he set about to write *The Great Gatsby*, but he implied an understanding of Conrad's special use of language to define themes when, in May, 1923, he began a book review with a quotation from Conrad's "Youth": "I did not know how good a man I was till then.... I remember my youth and the feeling that will never come back any more—the feeling that I could last forever, outlast the sea, the earth, and all men, ... the triumphant conviction of strength, the beat of life in the handful of dust, the glow in the heart that with every year grows dim, grows cold, grows small, and expires too soon—before life itself."[81] On the poetically rhythmical style of "Youth," Fitzgerald commented, "since that story I have found in nothing else even the echo of that lift and ring." This phrase, close to Conrad's own "shape and ring," suggests that Fitzgerald was fully aware of Conrad's theory of the use of language to extend meaning and, moreover, that he was probably attempting to follow in his own work Conrad's high, austere principles.

The closing lines of *The Great Gatsby* do echo the "lift and ring" of the passage Fitzgerald quoted from "Youth," and show how well Fitzgerald had mastered Conrad's art of magic suggestiveness:

> Most of the big shore places were closed now and there were hardly any lights except the shadowy, moving glow of a ferryboat across the Sound. And as the moon rose higher the inessential houses began to melt away until gradually I became aware of the old island here that flowered once for Dutch sailors' eyes—a fresh, green breast of the new world. Its vanished trees, the trees that had made way for Gatsby's house, had once pandered in whispers to the last and greatest of all human dreams; for a transitory enchanted moment man must have held his breath in the presence of this continent, compelled into an aesthetic contemplation he neither understood nor desired, face to face for the last time in history with something commensurate to his capacity for wonder.
>
> And as I sat there brooding on the old, unknown world, I thought of Gatsby's wonder when he first picked

out the green light at the end of Daisy's dock. He had come a long way to this blue lawn, and his dream must have seemed so close that he could hardly fail to grasp it. He did not know that it was already behind him, somewhere back in that vast obscurity beyond the city, where the dark fields of the republic rolled on under the night.

Gatsby believed in the green light, the orgastic future that year by year recedes before us. It eluded us then, but that's no matter—to-morrow we will run faster, stretch out our arms farther.... And one fine morning—

So we beat on, boats against the current, borne back ceaselessly into the past (217–18).

This passage—a "perfect blending of form and substance"—becomes more and more rhythmical simultaneously with the gradual expansion of the significance of Gatsby's dream. There is first the identification of his dream with the dream of those who discovered and settled the American continent—the "last and greatest of all human dreams"; there is next the association of Gatsby's dream with the dream of Modern America, lost somewhere in the "vast obscurity" of the "dark fields of the republic"; there is finally the poignant realization that all of these dreams are one and inseparable and forever without our grasp, not because of a failure of will or effort but rather because the dream is in reality a vision of the receding and irrecoverable, past. Nick Carraway's discovery is close to Marlow's knowledge in "Youth": they both sense "a feeling that will never come back any more," they both watch with an acute sense of tragedy "the glow in the heart" grow dim. At the end of *My Ántonia* Jim Burden could assert that he and Ántonia "possessed" the "precious, the incommunicable past"; the very fact that he felt the compulsion to commit that past to a written record suggests that he felt insecure in its possession. It was Nick's discovery that the past cannot be "possessed"; he had watched Gatsby searching for a past (a "past" that had not even had a momentary existence, that was the invention of his imagination) and, ultimately, finding death in its stead.

The green light at the end of Buchanan's dock will draw us on forever—but we shall never possess our Daisy, for she is a vision that really doesn't exist. Nick Carraway sees the green light when he catches his first brief glimpse of his neighbor; he sees Gatsby standing on his lawn, stretching his arms toward the dark water that separates East Egg from West Egg—Daisy from himself. When Nick looks out across the water, there is nothing visible "except a single green light, minute and far away, that might have been the end of a dock" (26). The green light, the contemporary signal which peremptorily summons the traveler on his way, serves well as the symbol for man in hurried pursuit of a beckoning but ever-elusive dream. And, if Gatsby's dream has particular application to America, as Lionel Trilling has suggested, probably no better symbol than the green light could be used for America's restless, reckless pursuit of the "American Dream."[82]

Notes

79. Fitzgerald, "Letters to Friends," *The Crack-Up*, p. 270.
80. Conrad, *The Nigger of the Narcissus*, p. xiii.
81. Fitzgerald, "Under Fire," *op. cit.*, p. 715.
82. Lionel Trilling, "Introduction," *The Great Gatsby* (New York: New Directions, 1945), p. viii.

SCOTT DONALDSON ON GATSBY AND THE HISTORICAL ANTECEDENTS FOR GATSBY

These ingredients—the unsuccessful quest, the loss of illusions—Fitzgerald blended into his greatest novel. "The whole idea of Gatsby," as he put it, "is the unfairness of a poor young man not being able to marry a girl with money." Gatsby really is a poor boy. As a child of poverty Jimmy Gatz grew up with Horatio Alger visions of attaining wealth and happiness and, therefore, the golden girl that Nick Carraway, the voice of Fitzgerald's rational self, can only scoff at. He also is gullible enough to believe that the possession of wealth will enable him to vault over the middle class into a position of social eminence. He does not see—he never sees—that he does not belong in Tom and Daisy Buchanan's world. Fitzgerald sees, all right. He's in the middle class with Nick, looking down at Gatsby and up at the Buchanans with mingled disapproval and admiration, both ways.

Perspective makes all the difference here. As Henry Dan Piper has noted, Fitzgerald invariably wrote about the rich from a middle class point of view. If his work seemed preoccupied with money, that was because money was a preoccupation of the middle class. There stands Fitzgerald outside the ballroom, nose pressed to the window while the dancers swirl about inside. But this is no Stella Dallas, washerwoman, watching her daughter married to the rich boy. For Fitzgerald has been inside the ballroom and hopes to be there again; this is only a dance to which he has not been invited. Then he walks downtown to sneer at the lower classes, who smell bad and talk funny and put on airs when they come into a bit of money. This rather sniffy attitude toward the poor emerges most powerfully in Fitzgerald's first two novels, and survives in *The Great Gatsby* through Nick's snobbery.

What *Gatsby* does, magnificently well, is to show the way love is affected by social class in the United States. One early reviewer complained about Fitzgerald's attributing Gatsby's passion for Daisy to her superior social status. That was nonsense, the reviewer objected: "Daisy might have been a cash girl or a mill hand and made as deep a mark—it is Carmen and Don Jose over again."

But this is not opera, and one lesson of Fitzgerald's book is that love becomes degrading when it roams too far across class lines. Let the fences down and God knows who will start rutting with whom. Tom Buchanan's brutality to Myrtle, together with her pitiful attempt at imitating upper class speech and behavior, make their party and their affair almost entirely sordid. On the surface it seems like the same situation in reverse with Daisy Buchanan and Gatsby. On the day of their reunion after nearly five years, Gatsby shows Daisy his garish house and produces resident pianist Klipspringer for a little afternoon music. Leaping to the conclusion that a casual copulation is imminent, Klipspringer first plays "The Love Nest," then "Ain't We Got Fun?" But he misunderstands. The difference between the two affairs derives from the strength of Gatsby's imagination. He is a parvenu, certainly, and it may be as Nick says that he had no real right to take Daisy since he lets her think he comes from "much the same stratum as herself," but in the meantime he has so idealized her as to make their relationship seem almost chaste.

(...)

While Daisy was obviously modeled on Ginevra King, Fitzgerald originally based the figure of Gatsby on a stock manipulator he'd encountered in Great Neck and then let the character gradually change into himself. "Gatsby was never quite real to me," he admitted. "His original served for a good enough exterior until about the middle of the book he grew thin and I began to fill him with my emotional life."

Fitzgerald did not really *know* the model for the early Gatsby, actually or imaginatively, and kept him off center stage until page 47, more than one-fourth of the novel's length. Before his appearance this Gatsby is propped up with rumors. He's the nephew of the Kaiser, it's thought, or he'd been a German spy in the war. One girl has heard that Gatsby went to Oxford, but doubts it. Another has heard that he's killed a man, and believes it. There's a natural letdown when this mystery man turns out to be—so it seems at first—only another *nouveau riche* who drives a too-ornate cream-colored "circus wagon," wears pink suits, and takes unseemly pride in the number and variety of his shirts. He also recites for Nick's benefit a highly improbable tale about his distinguished origins and colorful past, which included—so he says—living "like a young rajah in all the capitals of Europe" while collecting rubies, "hunting big game, painting a little ... and trying to forget something very sad that had happened to me long ago." It's all Nick can do to keep from laughing, but the story continues. Gatsby had gone off to war, where he'd tried "very hard" to dies but had instead fought so valiantly that "every Allied government" had decorated him.

This Gatsby is almost totally inept in dealing with social situations. His lavish parties are monuments to bad taste and conspicuous display; he thinks them splendid gatherings of the best and brightest. Moreover, he does not know when he is not wanted. Tom Buchanan, Mr. Sloane, and a lady friend stop off at his house during a horseback ride one day, and the lady invites Gatsby and Nick to come to dinner that evening. Nick at once realized that Mr. Sloane opposes this plan and politely declines, but Gatsby, eager to mingle with the plutocrats, accepts. While he's upstairs changing, they ride off.

This Gatsby "represented everything," Nick says, for which he feels "an unaffected scorn." Even when he tells Gatsby, on their last meeting, that he's "worth the whole damn bunch put together," Nick continues to disapprove of him on a social level. So does Fitzgerald. Gatsby has redeeming qualities, however. (If he did not, the novel would amount to nothing more than the most obvious satire.) Parts of his fantastic story turn out to be true. He *had* been a war hero, and has the medal from Montenegro to prove it. He *had* actually attended Oxford—for five months, as a postwar reward for military service, and produces a photograph in evidence. Above all, there was nothing phony or insincere about his dream of Daisy.

The power of Gatsby's imagination made him great. Parvenu though he was, he possessed "an extraordinary gift for hope, a romantic readiness" such as Nick had never found in anyone else. He even brought part of his dream to life. "The truth was that Jay Gatsby of West Egg, Long Island, sprang from his Platonic conception of himself." The seventeen-year-old James Gatz invented just the kind of Jay Gatsby that a poor boy from the cold shores of Lake Superior was likely to invent: a man of fabulous wealth, like the Dan Cody who lifted him from the lake and installed him on his dazzling yacht. In the service of Cody and Mammon and by whatever devious means, Gatsby had won through to wealth. To fulfill his dream it remained only to capture the golden girl, the king's daughter (the *Kings'* daughter) he had idealized in his mind. He had come close during the war, but Daisy had married Tom (and produced a little girl in whose existence Gatsby can barely bring himself to believe, until he is confronted with her in reality) and so sullied the purity of the dream.

To restore his ideal, Gatsby attempts to obliterate time and return to that moment in Louisville when as they kissed "Daisy blossomed for him like a flower and the incarnation was complete." Nick warns Gatsby that he cannot repeat the past, but he cries incredulously, "Why of course you can!" All that's required is for Daisy to tell Tom that she had never for one moment loved him, that she had never loved anyone but Gatsby. Then the impurity would be scrubbed away, and they could "go back to Louisville and be married from her house— just as if it were five years ago." But Daisy fails him. In the confrontation scene at the Plaza, she cannot bring herself to repudiate Tom entirely.

> "Oh, you want too much!" she cried to Gatsby. "I love you now—isn't that enough? I can't help what's past." She began to sob helplessly. "I did love him once—but I loved you too."
>
> Gatsby's eyes opened and closed.
>
> "You loved me too?" he repeated.

Even then, Gatsby refuses to give up his dream. "I don't think she ever loved him," he tells Nick the next morning. Tom had bullied her into saying that she had. Or perhaps, he concedes, she'd "loved him for a minute, when they were first married— and loved me more even then, do you see?" In any case, Gatsby adds, "It was just personal."

For Gatsby, the dream itself mattered far more than the person in whom the dream found expression. Toward the end Nick keeps insisting that Gatsby must have given up his dream, but there is no evidence that he did. He was still waiting for Daisy's phone call when the man from the ashheaps came calling instead.

Fitzgerald transferred to Gatsby both a situation from his own emotional life—the unsuccessful pursuit of the golden girl—and an attitude toward that quest. Like Gatsby and the sad young men of his best love stories, Fitzgerald was remarkable for the "colossal vitality" of his capacity for illusion. "I am always searching for the perfect love," he told Laura Guthrie in 1935. Was that because he'd had it as a young man? "No, I never had it," the answered. "I was searching then too." Such a search worked to prevent him from committing himself fully to any one person, for, as common sense dictated and his fiction illustrated, there could be no such thing as the perfect love, up close.

JOYCE A. ROWE ON GATSBY'S RELATIONSHIP WITH NICK

That Gatsby is not just the mythic embodiment of an American type but personifies the outline of our national consciousness is demonstrated by his structural relation to the other characters and, in particular, to the narrator, Nick Carraway.

Despite differences of class and taste, despite their apparent mutually antagonistic purposes, all the characters in this book are defined by their nostalgia for and sense of betrayal by some lost, if only dimly apprehended promise in their past—a sense of life's possibilities toward which only Gatsby has retained the ingenuous faith and energy of the true seeker. It is in the difference between vision and sight, between the longing for self-transcendence and the lust for immediate gain—for sexual, financial, or social domination—that Nick, his chronicler and witness, finds the moral distinction which separates Gatsby from the "foul dust" of the others who float in his wake. And this moral dichotomy runs through the structure of the entire work. For the rapacious nature of each of the others, whether crude, desperate, arrogant or false, is finally shown to be a function of their common loss of vision, their blurred or displaced sense of possibilities—punningly symbolized In the enormous empty retinas of the occulist-wag, Dr T.J. Eckleburg. Thus Gatsby and those who eddy around him are, reciprocally, positive and negative images of one another; but whether faithless or true all are doomed by the wasteful, self-deluding nature of the longing which controls their lives and which when it falls leaves its adherents utterly naked and alone, "contiguous to nothing."

However, Nick's insight into the distinction between Gatsby and others does not free him from his own involvement in the world he observes. His acute awareness of his own self-division (toward Gatsby as toward all the others) turns out to be the mirror inversion of his subject's unconscious one; it accounts for the sympathetic bond between them. And Just as Gatsby's ingenuous self-dissociation is the ground of his faith that the moral complexity of the world can be subdued to his imaginative vision (Daisy's feelings for Tom are only a case of the "personal"), so Nick's self-division leads him to ultimately reject the world ("I wanted no more ... privileged glimpses into the human heart"). They are twin poles of All or Nothing—Gatsby's hope is Nick's despair.

Nick's kinship to Gatsby is established in the prologue, where his own version of "infinite hope"—the capacity to reserve judgment—is implicitly contrasted with Gatsby's "extraordinary gift for hope." This latter is not, says Nick, in a self-deprecating reference, a matter of any "flabby impressionability," but of a romantic readiness such as he has never found in any other person "and which it is not likely I shall ever find again." The phrase tells us that Nick too is a seeker, that the strength of Gatsby's romantic energy resonates against Nick's own muted but responsive sensibility. Indeed, Nick's most immediately distinguishing trait, his consciousness of the flux of time as a series of intense, irrecoverable moments, is keyed to a romantic pessimism whose melancholy note is struck on his thirtieth birthday, when he envisions his future as a burden of diminishing returns leading inexorably to loneliness, enervation, and death.

Moreover, it is Nick's own confused responsiveness to his cousin's sexual power and charm that allows him subsequently to understand Gatsby's equation of Daisy with all that is most desirable under the heavens—ultimately with the siren song of the American continent. Nick cannot help but be compelled by the buoyant vitality which surrounds her and the glowing sound of her "low, thrilling voice," which sings with "a promise that she had done gay,' exciting things just a while since and that there were gay exciting things hovering in the next hour." But, as the shadow of his double, Nick's response to Daisy is qualified by his discomforting awareness of the illusory and deceptive in her beauty. Her smirking insincerity, her banal chatter, the alluring whiteness of her expensive clothes—most of all, the languid boredom which enfolds her life—suggest a willing captivity, a lazy self-submission to a greater power than her own magical charms: the extraordinary wealth and physical arrogance that enable Tom Buchanan to dominate her. And Nick's visceral dislike for the man Daisy has given herself to, fanned by his intellectual and moral scorn for Tom's crude attempt to master "ideas" as he does horses and women, allies him with, as it prefigures, Gatsby's bland disregard of Tom as a factor in Daisy's existence.

JAMES L.W. WEST III ON THE ORIGINAL TITLE'S SIGNIFICANCE TO THEME

Trimalchio, a freed slave who has grown wealthy, hosts a lavish banquet in one of the best-known chapters of the *Satyricon* by Petronius (*c*. AD 27–66). In translations, the chapter is usually entitled "The Party at Trimalchio's" or "Trimalchio's Feast"; it is one of the best accounts of domestic revelry to survive from the reign of the emperor Nero. The chapter is narrated by Encolpius, an observer and recorder rather than a participant.

Banquet scenes were conventions of classical literature (e.g., the *Symposia* of Plato and Xenophon). They were occasions for mild jesting and for conversations about art, literature, and philosophy. Trimalchio's party is a parody of this convention: most of the guests are inebriated and are disdainful of learning; their crude talk, in colloquial Latin, is largely about money and possessions.

Trimalchio himself is old and unattractive, bibulous and libidinous. His house, though, is spacious; his dining-room contains an impressively large water-clock; his servants are dressed in elaborate costumes. The banquet he hosts is ostentatious, with entertainments carefully rehearsed and staged. There are numerous courses of food and drink and several rounds of gifts for the guests, many of whom do not know Trimalchio and speak slightingly of him when he leaves the room.

The banquet becomes progressively more vinous; it ends with a drunken Trimalchio feigning death atop a mound of pillows, his hired trumpeters blaring a funeral march. The noise brings the city's fire crew; they kick in the door and cause chaos with water and axes. Encolpius and his friends escape into the night without bidding farewell to their host.

Scott Donaldson on Possessions and Character in *The Great Gatsby*

When T.S. Eliot wrote F. Scott Fitzgerald that *The Great Gatsby* seemed to him "the first step that American fiction has taken since Henry James," he linked the two writers as social novelists in whose work the issue is joined between innocence and experience, between those who repudiate artificial limitations and those who recognize and respect the envelope of circumstances, between the individual yearning for independence and the society forever reining him in. Fitzgerald, like James, understood that the pursuit of independence was doomed from the start. Try though they might, Fitzgerald's characters find it impossible to throw off "the cluster of appurtenances" and invent themselves anew. That is the lesson, or one of the lessons, of *The Great Gatsby*.

One's house, one's clothes: they do express one's self, and no one more than Jay Gatsby. It is in good part because of the clothes he wears that Tom Buchanan is able to undermine him as a competitor for Daisy. "'An Oxford man!' [Tom] was incredulous. 'Like hell he is! He wears a pink suit.'" Yes, and for tea a white flannel suit with silver shirt and gold tie. And drives a monstrously long cream-colored car, a veritable "circus wagon," in Tom's damning phrase. And inhabits a huge mansion where he throws lavish, drunken parties "for the world and its mistress." Given an opportunity, Gatsby consistently errs in the direction of ostentation. His clothes, his car, his house, his parties—all brand him as newly rich, unschooled in the social graces and sense of superiority ingrained not only in Tom Buchanan but also in Nick Carraway.

(...)

Married to the pallid proprietor of a gas station in the ash-heaps, Myrtle must cross a vast social divide to reach the territory of the upper class. Her smoldering sensuality enables her to attract Tom Buchanan, and in the small apartment on West 158th Street that Tom rents as a place of assignation, she pitifully attempts to put on airs. But what Myrtle buys and plans to buy during the Sunday party in Chapter Two tellingly reveals her status. She aims for extravagance, but has had no experience with it.

When Myrtle and Tom and Nick Carraway, who has been commandeered by Tom to "meet his girl," reach Grand Central Station, Myrtle buys a copy of the gossip magazine *Town Tattle* at the newsstand and "some cold cream and a small flask of perfume" from the drug store's cosmetics counter. Next she exercises her discrimination by letting several taxicabs go by before selecting a lavender-colored one—not quite a circus wagon, but unseemly in its showy color. Then she stops the cab in order to "get one of those dogs" for the apartment from a sidewalk salesman. This man resembles John D. Rockefeller and is, like him, less than straightforward in his business dealings. He claims that the puppy he fetches from his basket is a male Airedale, and he demands ten dollars for it. In fact the dog is a mongrel bitch, and in a gesture Myrtle must have found wonderfully cavalier, Tom pays the inflated price with a characteristic insult. "Here's your money. Go and buy ten more dogs with it."

Myrtle becomes emboldened in her pretensions amid the surroundings of their hideously overcrowded apartment. Under the inspiration of whiskey, a private interlude with Tom, and her third costume change of the day—this time into "an elaborate afternoon dress of cream-colored chiffon" that rustles as she sweeps across the room she assumes an "impressive hauteur." Complimented on the dress, Myrtle cocks an eyebrow disdainfully. The dress, she announces, is just a crazy old thing she slips on when she doesn't care how she looks. The eyebrows go up again when the elevator boy is slow in bringing ice. "These people!" she declares. "You have to keep after them all the time." Waxing ever more expansive, Myrtle promises to give Mrs. McKee the dress off her back. She's "got to get another one tomorrow" anyway, as but one item on a shopping list that includes "[a] massage and a wave and a collar for the dog and one of those cute little ashtrays where you touch a spring, and a wreath with a black silk bow" for her mother's grave: "I got to write down a list so I won't forget all the things I got to do." The "I got" idiom betrays Myrtle's origins. The list itself—with its emphasis on ashes and dust—foreshadows her eventual demise.

Such reminders of Myrtle's unfortunate position as Tom's mistress and victim are required to prevent her from becoming a merely comic figure. As it is, Fitzgerald skewers her affectations with obvious relish. On arrival at the apartment house, he writes, Myrtle casts "a regal home, coming glance around the neighborhood." Once inside, she flounces around the place, her voice transformed into "a high mincing shout" and her laughter becoming progressively more artificial. Tom brings her crashing to earth when Mr. McKee, the photographer, comments that he'd "like to do more work" for the wealthy residents of Long Island. With a shout of laughter, Tom proposes that McKee secure a letter of introduction from Myrtle to her husband so that McKee could take photographs of him: "George B. Wilson at the Gasoline Pump," perhaps. Neither Chester McKee nor Myrtle Wilson, it is clear, will gain access to the privileged precincts of East Egg. In fact, when Myrtle goes so far as to repeat Daisy's name, Tom breaks her nose with a slap of his open hand.

Among Myrtle's purchases, the dog of indeterminate breeding best symbolizes her own situation. She is, for Tom, a possession to be played with, fondled, and in due course ignored. "Tom's got some woman in New York," Jordan says by way of breaking the news to Nick, who is bewildered by the locution. "Got some woman?" he repeats blankly. In her politically and grammatically incorrect manner, Mrs. McKee understands the concept perfectly. If Chester hadn't come along at the right time, she tells Myrtle, the "little kyke" who'd been after her for years would "of got me sure." In the same fashion, Myrtle wants to "get" a dog for the apartment. "They're nice to have—a dog."

The connection between Myrtle and the dog as creatures to be kept under restraint is underlined by the collar she plans to buy, and by the expensive leather-and-silver leash her husband discovers on her bureau, arousing his suspicions. During Nick's final meeting with Tom, Fitzgerald twice evokes the dog comparison. According to Tom, who does not know Daisy was driving at the time, Gatsby deserved to die, for he "ran over Myrtle like you'd run over a dog and never even stopped his car." And Tom himself cried like a baby, he bathetically insists, when he went to give up the flat and saw "the box of dog biscuits sitting there on the sideboard." For the times, Tom was not unusual in regarding women as objects to be possessed— either temporarily, as in the case of Myrtle, or permanently, if like Daisy they warrant such maintenance through their beauty and background and way of presenting themselves to the world.

(...)

Jay Gatsby, son of Henry Gatz before he reimagines himself into a son of God, has risen from much the same stratum as Myrtle Wilson. The limitations of this background finally make it impossible for him to win the enduring love of Daisy Fay Buchanan. And, like Myrtle, he is guilty of a crucial error in judgment. They are alike unwilling or unable to comprehend that it is not money alone that matters, but money combined with secure social position. In the attempt to transcend their status through a show of possessions, they are undone by the lack of cultivation that drives them to buy the wrong things. At that point they fall victim to what Ronald Berman calls "the iron laws of social distinction."

The sheer exhibitionism of Myrtle's three-dress afternoon prefigures what we are soon to see in Gatsby's clothes closet. Still more than him, she is under the sway of appearances. On successive pages, she describes first how disillusioned she was to discover that her husband had married her in a borrowed suit, and second how thrilled she was to encounter Tom Buchanan on the commuter train in his "dress suit and patent leather shoes." When his white shirt front presses against her arm, she is erotically overcome.

In depicting the unhappy end of Myrtle Wilson and Jay Gatsby, Fitzgerald was painting a broad-brush portrait of his own experience. Near the novel's close, Nick condemns Tom and Daisy as careless people who "smashed up things and creatures and then retreated back into their money or their vast carelessness or whatever it was that kept them together." In this bitter passage, Fitzgerald is writing about himself as well as the characters. "The whole idea of Gatsby," as he put it, "is the unfairness of a poor young man not being able to marry a girl with money. The theme comes up again and again because I lived it." Lived it with Ginevra King, who serves as the principal model for Daisy, and very nearly again with Zelda Sayre.

In rejecting Scott as a suitor, Ginevra made it painfully clear that there were boundaries he could not cross. Two quotations from Fitzgerald's ledger, recorded after visits to Ginevra's home in Lake Forest, document his disappointment in love. The better known of these, "Poor boys shouldn't think of marrying rich girls," probably came from Ginevra's father. Fitzgerald naturally took the remark to heart, as directed at him. But the second quotation—a rival's offhand "I'm going to take Ginevra home in my electric"—may have hurt just as much, for Scott had no car at all with which to compete for her company. She came from a more exalted social universe, one he could visit but not belong to. In an interview about their relationship more than half a century later, Ginevra maintained that she never regarded young Fitzgerald as marriageable material, never "singled him out as anything special."

On the most banal level, The Great Gatsby documents the truism that money can't buy you love, or at least not the tainted money Gatsby acquires in his campaign to take Daisy away from her husband. It would have been difficult for him to compete with Tom's resources, in any event. Nick describes the Buchanans as "enormously wealthy," and Tom himself as a notorious spendthrift. When he and Daisy moved from Lake Forest (the location is significant) to East Egg, for example, he brought along a string of polo ponies. "It was hard to realize that a man in my own generation was wealthy enough to do that," Nick observes.

Part of Gatsby's dream is to turn back the clock and marry Daisy in a conventional wedding, but there too he would have been hard put to equal Tom's extravagance. When Tom married Daisy in June 1919, he brought a hundred guests in four private railway cars? It took an entire floor of the hotel to put them up. As a wedding gift he presented Daisy with "a string of pearls valued at three hundred and fifty thousand dollars"—a tremendously impressive sum in 1919 (or any other time), but nonetheless marked down from "seven hundred and fifty thousand dollars" in *Trimalchio*, the early version of the novel Fitzgerald sent Maxwell Perkins in the fall of 1924. He must have decided that the higher figure was beyond belief.

In tying up the threads, Nick offers a final glimpse of Tom outside a jewelry store on Fifth Avenue. As they part, Tom goes into the store "to buy a pearl necklace" for Daisy or some other conquest, "or perhaps only a pair of cuff buttons," a suggestion that there is something as unsavory about Tom as about Meyer Wolfsheim, the man who fixed the World Series.

Even discounting how much there is of it, Tom's "old money" has a power beyond any that Gatsby can command. His wealth and background win the battle for Daisy, despite his habitual infidelities—an outcome that seems not only grossly unfair but morally wrong, for another point Fitzgerald is making is that if you have enough money and position you can purchase immunity from punishment. Actions have consequences, as we remind our children, but some people can evade those consequences. Gatsby probably avoids prosecution for bootlegging and bond-rigging by distributing his resources on a *quid pro quo* basis, and rather callously applies that principle to his personal life as well. Once he did the police commissioner a favor; now he can break the speed limit. Nick arranges a meeting with Daisy. Gatsby offers him a business connection.

Gatsby's evasions, however, are nothing compared to those of the Buchanans. As Nick reluctantly shakes Tom's hand at the end, he comments that it seemed silly not to; it was like shaking hands with a child. But Tom and Daisy are not children playing innocent games. Daisy commits vehicular manslaughter, then compounds the felony by letting others think Gatsby was driving. In directing Wilson to West Egg, Tom escapes the wrath he knows should be directed at him and becomes an accessory to murder. In a magazine article published the year prior to Gatsby, Fitzgerald inveighed against children of privilege who drive automobiles recklessly, knowing that Dad will bribe the authorities should they happen to run over anyone when drunk. And in "The Rich Boy," published the year after the novel, his protagonist nonchalantly drives lovers to suicide without feeling the slightest stab of guilt. The message in all these cases would seem to be that if you have the right background, you can get away with murder. In Gatsby itself, the two characters who fall in love above their station pay with their lives for their presumption, while Tom and Daisy assuage any discomfort they may feel over cold chicken and ale. It is a double standard with a vengeance.

So finally even Nick Carraway, who was Daisy Fay's cousin and Jordan Baker's lover and Tom Buchanan's classmate at Yale, concludes that Gatsby was all right, that he was worth "the whole damn bunch put together." The commendation means a great deal coming from Nick, who is something of a snob and who disapproved of Gatsby from the beginning, largely because of his impudence in breaching class barriers. Gatsby met Daisy, Nick tells us, only through the "colossal accident" of the war. Knowing he did not belong in her world, he "took what he could get, ravenously and unscrupulously ... took [Daisy] because he had no real right to touch her hand." Gatsby's later idealization of Daisy and their love redeems him, however, and he dies protecting her by his silence. He no more deserves to be shot than Myrtle deserves to be struck by a speeding car. Get mixed up with the Buchanans, and you end up dead.

Works by F. Scott Fitzgerald

This Side of Paradise, 1920.
Flappers and Philosophers, 1920.
The Beautiful and the Damned, 1922.
Tales of the Jazz Age, 1922.
The Vegetable, 1923.
The Great Gatsby, 1925.
All The Sad Young Men, 1926.
Tender is the Night, 1934.
Taps at Reveille, 1935.
The Last Tycoon, 1941.
The Crack Up, 1945.

Annotated Bibliography

As a scholarly topic, F. Scott Fitzgerald and *The Great Gatsby* are nearly comparable to Shakespeare in terms of the amount of work written about them. Virtually no other American writer has yielded the volume of criticism as has Fitzgerald, so any short bibliography is bound to be incomplete. Much of the book-length studies in the last twenty years have considered Fitzgerald writ large—cultural impact, his reputation abroad, his connections and influence with other writers, and the like. Papers on *The Great Gatsby* have not abated, however. Each year sees a few dozen papers appear in journals, dealing with the novel itself or comparing aspects of the novel with other works. For that reason, we note that one of the volumes here has a more comprehensive bibliography on Fitzgerald, for those interested in the wider arena of work on both the novel as well as the writer.

Berman, Ronald. "*The Great Gatsby* and the Twenties," in *The Cambridge Companion to F. Scott Fitzgerald*, ed. Ruth Prigozy (New York: Cambridge University Press, 2002): pp. 79–94.

Berman's essay reveals the latest scholarship on the historical, cultural, and thematic context of the novel. Prigozy also includes in the back of the volume a lengthy bibliography on Fitzgerald in general, compiled with the aid of Jackson R. Bryer.

———. "*The Great Gatsby*" and Fitzgerald's World of Ideas (Tuscaloosa: University of Alabama Press, 1997).

Berman talks about how the novel contained incarnations of Fitzgerald's views, most notably on idealism and the American dream, and the failure of both.

———. "*The Great Gatsby*" in Modern Times (Urbana: University of Illinois Press, 1994).

As does his essay noted above, Berman's book places the novel in historical, political, and cultural context.

Bruccoli, Matthew J., ed. *New Essays on "The Great Gatsby,"* (New York: Cambridge University Press, 1985).

Containing essays by a number of Fitzgerald authorities, collected by the man who was seen as a "Fitzgerald industry" for decades, the collection provides a useful overview of the novel in the context of literary achievement of the twentieth century, and connects Fitzgerald to other writers and movements.

————. *Some Sort of Epic Grandeur: The Life of F. Scott Fitzgerald* (New York: Harcourt Brace Jovanovich, 1981).

While still referred to as the definitive biography by the scholar long considered the leading figure on Fitzgerald, the biography tends to lionize the writer, and has led others to attempt to "balance" the appreciation of Fitzgerald. See Donaldson.

————, ed. *"The Great Gatsby": A Facsimile of the Manuscript* (Washington, D.C.: Microcard Editions Books, 1973), et al.

Bruccoli has edited a number of collections of Fitzgerald manuscripts (of which the above-referenced volume is only one). Through his work collecting the materials, readers can examine notes and emendations by Fitzgerald himself, as well as by Maxwell Perkins, to gain insight into the author's creative process.

Bryer, Jackson R. *F. Scott Fitzgerald: The Critical Reception* (New York: Burt Franklin, 1978).

One of the most important scholars in Fitzgerald studies and in bibliographical studies in general, Bryer includes in his study a lengthy consideration of the initial and eventual impact of *The Great Gatsby.*

Donaldson, Scott. *Critical Essays on F. Scott Fitzgerald's "The Great Gatsby"* (Boston: G.K. Hall & Co., 1984).

The collection includes more than twenty different critics weighing in on matters ranging from Fitzgerald's creative process for the novel to its overarching themes and the American mythology it both used and helped to create. This volume also includes a number of letters from Fitzgerald to Perkins and other writers.

———. *Fool for Love: F. Scott Fitzgerald* (New York: Congdon and Weed, 1983).

While some consider this biography of Fitzgerald to present him in a negative light, it is useful when compared with Bruccoli's more positive bias, and it builds on Bruccoli's insights regarding the composition of the novel.

Kuehl, John and Jackson R. Bryer, ed. *Dear Scott/Dear Max: The Fitzgerald-Perkins Correspondence* (New York: Charles Scribner's Sons, 1971).

Important edited collection of the letters between Fitzgerald and his famous editor, Maxwell Perkins. Though they focus on the entirety of the relationship, there is still a very significant and illuminating section of letters dealing with the revision of *The Great Gatsby*, and many letters that reveal much about Fitzgerald's writing habits and opinions. The vast majority of work done on *The Great Gatsby* quotes from this source.

Long, Robert E. *The Achieving of "The Great Gatsby"* (Lewisburg: Bucknell University Press, 1979).

Long examines the development of Fitzgerald's writing technique. He argues that the book showed a stylistic maturity allowing full expression of Fitzgerald's ideas, and due to that achievement, influenced and defined literature in and for the 1920s.

Stern, Milton. "The Great Gatsby: A Willingness of the Heart," in *The Golden Moment: The Novels of F. Scott Fitzgerald*, by Milton R. Stern (Urbana: University of Illinois Press, 1970): pp. 161–288.

The book as a whole centers on a critical look at Fitzgerald's themes and how they result in the narrative structures in his novels. The chapter on *The Great Gatsby* has been consistently cited in subsequent Fitzgerald scholarship.

West, James L.W. III. *The Perfect Hour: The Romance of F. Scott Fitzgerald and Ginevra King, His First Love* (New York: Random House, 2005).

Based on personal writings of Ginevra King only recently made available, this study reconsiders the role Ginevra played in the formation of Fitzgerald's female characters, most notably Daisy Buchanan.

———, ed. *Trimalchio*, by F. Scott Fitzgerald (Cambridge: Cambridge University Press, 2002).

Trimalchio is the complete draft of the novel Fitzgerald sent to Maxwell Perkins. Though not a great novel, as West points out, it is still very good, and it contains the bones for what would become *The Great Gatsby*, and is a useful insight regarding authorial process and the relation between Fitzgerald and Perkins.

Contributors

Harold Bloom is Sterling Professor of the Humanities at Yale University. He is the author of 30 books, including *Shelley's Mythmaking* (1959), *The Visionary Company* (1961), *Blake's Apocalypse* (1963), *Yeats* (1970), *A Map of Misreading* (1975), *Kabbalah and Criticism* (1975), *Agon: Toward a Theory of Revisionism* (1982), *The American Religion* (1992), *The Western Canon* (1994), and *Omens of Millennium: The Gnosis of Angels, Dreams, and Resurrection* (1996). *The Anxiety of Influence* (1973) sets forth Professor Bloom's provocative theory of the literary relationships between the great writers and their predecessors. His most recent books include *Shakespeare: The Invention of the Human* (1998), a 1998 National Book Award finalist, *How to Read and Why* (2000), *Genius: A Mosaic of One Hundred Exemplary Creative Minds* (2002), *Hamlet: Poem Unlimited* (2003), *Where Shall Wisdom be Found* (2004), and *Jesus and Yahweh: The Names Divine* (2005). In 1999, Professor Bloom received the prestigious American Academy of Arts and Letters Gold Medal for Criticism. He has also received the International Prize of Catalonia, the Alfonso Reyes Prize of Mexico, and the Hans Christian Andersen Bicentennial Prize of Denmark.

Gabriel Welsch's short stories, poems, and reviews have appeared in *Georgia Review*, *Mid-American Review*, *Crab Orchard Review*, and *Cream City Review*. He regularly reviews literature for *Harvard Review*, *Missouri Review*, *Slope*, and *Small Press Review*. He received a Pennsylvania Council on the Arts Fellowship for Literature in fiction in 2003.

G. Thomas Tanselle is Senior Vice President of the John Simon Guggenheim Memorial Foundation. He has been President of the Bibliographical Society of America. He is the author of several of the most influential volumes on bibliographical and textual scholarship, including *A Rationale of Textual Criticism*,

Selected Studies in Bibliography, and *Textual Criticism and Scholarly Editing*. His *Guide to the Study of U.S. Imprints* is a basic guide to the study of American publishing history.

Jackson R. Bryer is Professor of English at the University of Maryland. He has written or edited over thirty books, including *The Critical Reputation of F. Scott Fitzgerald*; *F. Scott Fitzgerald in His Own Time*; *Dear Scott/Dear Max*; and *New Essays on F. Scott Fitzgerald's Neglected Stories*.

Matthew J. Bruccoli is the Emily Brown Jefferies Professor of English at the University of South Carolina. He is a noted Fitzgerald scholar and has edited more than 30 works on Fitzgerald.

Dan Seiters works at Southern Illinois University at Carbondale, and is the author as well of *Dastardly Dashing of Wee Expectations*.

John F. Callahan is Morgan S. Odell Professor of Humanities at Lewis and Clark College. He is the author of *In the African-American Grain: The Pursuit of Voice in 20th Century Black Fiction*; and *The Illusions of a Nation: Myth and History in the Novels of F. Scott Fitzgerald*.

Milton R. Stern is Professor of English and Distinguished Alumni Professor Emeritus at the University of Connecticut and the author of *The Golden Moment: The Novels of F. Scott Fitzgerald*; *The Fine Hammered Steel of Herman Melville*; *F. Scott Fitzgerald's "The Great Gatsby": Some American Cultural Dimensions*, and other books.

James E. Miller, Jr., is the Helen A. Regenstein Professor of Literature Emeritus at the University of Chicago. He is the author of *Theory of Fiction: Henry James*; *The American Quest for a Supreme Fiction: Whitman's Legacy in the Personal Epic*; *Heritage of American Literature*, and other titles.

Scott Donaldson is the author of *Hemingway vs. Fitzgerald: The Rise and Fall of a Literary Friendship; John Cheever: A Biography; By Force of Will: The Life and Art of Ernest Hemingway; Archibald MacLeish: An American Life;* and *Poet in America: Winfield Townley Scott.*

Joyce A. Rowe is a Professor of English at Fordham University and the author of *Equivocal Endings in Classic American Novels.*

Ronald Berman is Professor of English Literature at the University of California, San Diego. He is the author of several books, among them *The Great Gatsby and Modern Times; The Great Gatsby and Fitzgerald's World of Ideas; Fitzgerald, Hemingway, and the Twenties;* and *Fitzgerald's Intellectual Context.*

James L. W. West III is Sparks Professor of English at The Pennsylvania State University. He has held fellowships from the Guggenheim Foundation, the National Humanities Center, and the National Endowment for the Humanities, and has been a Fulbright scholar to England and Belgium. He is the author of *William Styron: A Life* and is general editor of the Cambridge Edition of the Works of F. Scott Fitzgerald.

Acknowledgments

G. Thomas Tanselle and Jackson R. Bryer, "*The Great Gatsby*: A Study in Literary Reputation," from *New Mexico Quarterly*, XXXIII (Winter 1963-64): pp. 409–425. Reprinted by permission.

Matthew Bruccoli, *Some Sort of Epic Grandure The Life of F. Scott Fitzgerald* (New York: Harcourt Brace Jovanovich, 1981): pp. 222–224. Reprinted by permission of the author.

Dan Seiters, *Image Patterns in the Novels of F. Scott Fitzgerald* (Ann Arbor: UMI Press, 1986): pp. 58–60, 64–67, 73–76. Used by permission.

Callahan, John F. From *The Illusions of a Nation: Myth and History in the Novels of F. Scott Fitzgerald*, (Urbana: University of Illinois Press, 1972): pp. 53-57. Reprinted by permission of the author.

Milton R. Stern, From *The Golden Moment: The Novels of F. Scott Fitzgerald*, (Urbana: University of Illinois Press, 1970): pp. 166–169, 170–173. Reprinted by permission of the author.

James E. Miller, *F. Scott Fitzgerald: His Art and His Technique* (New York: New York University Press, 1964): pp. 111, 114–115, 121–123. Reprinted by permission.

Scott Donaldson, *Fool for Love: F. Scott Fitzgerald* (New York: Congdon & Weed, 1983): pp. 105–106, 108–110. Reprinted by permission of the author.

Trimalchio, by F. Scott Fitzgerald (Cambridge: Cambridge University Press, 2002): pp. 190. Reprinted with the permission of Cambridge University Press.

"Possessions in The Great Gatsby," *The Southern Review* 37, 2 (Spring 2001): pp. 187–197. Reprinted by permission of the author. Biographer Scott Donaldson is editor of *Critical Essays on "The Great Gatsby"*.

Index

Characters in literary works are indexed by first name (if any), followed by the name of the work in parentheses